VIBRATIONS

How God Talks To Us

By
Anton Delgado

Order this book online at www.trafford.com
or email orders@trafford.com

Most Trafford titles are also available at major online book retailers.

Note for Librarians: A cataloguing record for this book is available from Library and Archives Canada at www.collectionscanada.ca/amicus/index-e.html

Printed in Victoria, BC, Canada.

ISBN: 978-1-4251-8163-5 (soft cover)
ISBN: 978-1-4251-8164-2 (eBook)

Our mission is to efficiently provide the world's finest, most comprehensive book publishing service, enabling every author to experience success. To find out how to publish your book, your way, and have it available worldwide, visit us online at www.trafford.com.

Trafford Rev. 05/17/2010

www.trafford.com

North America & international
toll-free: 1 888 232 4444 (USA & Canada)
phone: 250 383 6864 • fax:812 355 4082

CONTENTS

A Note from the Author

This book has the power of inducing a calm feeling, an emotional sense of well-being that can only come from being engulfed by the Holy Spirit and by reaching a higher level of consciousness that produces maturity in our spiritual awareness. It will make the readers sleepy, thus withdrawing them from the challenges of the world around them. When we are overcome by the Spirit, we will experience an enhancement of calmness throughout our subconscious and conscious mind, leaving behind our fast-paced American lifestyle. There will be no concern over job security, finances, weight, health or other worries that we might have. The Holy Spirit is an appeasement to our troubles, like an anesthetic. The information given here will give us the certainty that we are not alone with our struggles. However, the best way to read this book is by just opening it and letting the Holy Spirit guide you to whatever chapter He wants you to read.

God bless

PREFACE

I wrote this book with the intention of shouting that God is not One who alienates, but instead He is a liberator who makes individuals free with mature faith. He sculptures us with purity and passion that transforms us to an ecstatic closeness with His presence which develops into an intimate relationship. God is palpable and a concrete living person. Surprisingly, even in these days of a highly technological society we can seek Him, and in return, He will remove the silence and diffuseness of the clouds and shadows that cover His demonstrable realistic unfathomable mystery. God is the absolute value achieved in the highest of contemplative states. God is the only force capable of taking us out of our grounded physical life into the spiritual life. Living in the spirit will infuse us with the joy of God's presence. He will have the proper, fundamental answers for our hurts and tribulations. We will be confronted with our own mystery of our existence. Everything we have experienced in our lives will unravel in psychological terms explaining our destiny and fate. In the area of philosophy we will discover that after each milestone and experience there is recognition and accomplishment for the body of Christ. Being aware of our subconscious will help us into the great leap of conscious realization of the existence of the Almighty. The anthropological concept here is not to get caught in the absolute of humanity. Instead let us grant autonomy to our spiritual absolute which includes the physical world and the spiritual world. In the spirit, God is man's best friend. He will lead us to the infinite and inexhaustible path of goodness, acceptance, forgiveness and **hope.**

ACKNOWLEDGEMENTS

I want to thank first and foremost our Lord Jesus Christ for His guidance---for without Him, nothing is possible for Christians. I also want to thank two women who were very important in the making of this book. Without their help this book would just have been a dream: Pam Brown and Martha Lou Broaddus. My friends, who are also my customers, gave me support and encouragement. I appreciate their faith and belief that this book could be possible. I am also grateful for the constant support and love of my family and for the understanding of my dear husband for the absence of my full attention for more than the four years that it took me to write this book.

The Author, 2009

* * *

"Behold, I stand at the door and knock. If anyone hears My voice and opens the door, I will come in to him and dine with him, and he with Me. To him who overcomes I will grant to sit with Me on My throne, as I also overcame and sat down with My Father on His throne. He, who has an ear, let him hear what the Spirit says to the churches." Rev. 3:20-22

INTRODUCTION

This is a nondenominational book, a story of an ordinary person. The purpose is to share the phenomenal experience existing in the power of contemplative prayer which interchangeably relates to meditation and mysticism.

If we make ourselves aware of God's presence, He will offer intimacy and love that surpasses reasoning or explanation. Having a relationship with the Great God of the universe will enlighten us and make us receptive to His love, leading us to an intimacy difficult to fathom. We cannot exhaust or understand the meaning of His name, but we know His authority and power when we have communion with Him.

Anton is inspired by the Holy Spirit and her message is simple, that through meditation we can experience a higher consciousness which will expose us to the sensitivity of God's presence, giving us knowledge of His will. When the Holy Spirit implanted this assignment of writing a Christian book in her heart, knowing she was not knowledgeable about the Bible, her response was, "No, you have the wrong person. I am not a liturgical expert!" However, the Lord prevails and directs us to His path. Now she can testify what it is to submit to the Lord.

She realized His knowledge would be demonstrated more coming from a lay person so she agreed on this mission and became captivated with the Holy Spirit's information. Of course, going back to Bible history, the first group of apostles included only a couple of professional men: The physician Luke and the tax collector Matthew. The rest were ordinary men. Remembering this helped her understand, gave her confidence to trust the inner voice and believe that God; is in total control of us, the world and the universe. We should appreciate and comprehend God's effort to capture our human capacity, making us understand the mystery of His divine presence. He has the power to perform miracles as long as we stay in unity with each other in His Mystical Body, in His word. This does not mean we will not experience tribulation in our lives; it just means we will not be alone. He will remain with us in this imperfect world. He will help us walk on water, so to speak, and to come out of our difficulties without drowning. Society suffers from tribulation because people fail to restrain themselves adequately by not transgressing against God. Not practicing His laws or even exercising His laws without faith will bring consequences. No matter under what aspect we consider this problem, the fact stands that we will always find difficulties and tribulations in our life that cannot be solved or understood in time to prevent the occurrence of the transgression. This is precisely the reason that nobody is spared from exceedingly helping other human beings with their lives and **faith**.

Even John the Baptist made the mistake of doubting that Jesus was the Messiah when he was arrested and imprisoned. John sent his disciples to ask Jesus,

"Are You the Coming One, or do we look for another?" Matt. 11:3

How could he doubt when he himself witnessed the Holy Spirit manifest Himself as a dove that descended on Jesus and heard God' voice. Some of us are discouraged and disillusioned when we experience transgressions and failures. We feel disappointed and forgotten. We do not realize how important it is not to waver in our faith and stay focused on the word. John lost his head, but fortunately he had finished his mission.

"O thou of little faith, wherefore didst thou doubt?" Matt. 14:31

When we doubt our faith we lose God's protection that is extremely sensitive in the physical realm, because of our free will. The enemy does not lose an opportunity to take advantage of our weakness and he is always ready to attack and destroy us before we can finish our mission here on earth. The intent here is to realize how fortunate we are now to have the Holy Spirit within us after Jesus' ascension. *John 16:7* Our faith should not fluctuate or wander for a minute; it could be that the situation we are experiencing is for our benefit or somebody else's benefit. The point here is to learn to have an open mind in meditation and to become skilled in differentiating our thoughts from **God's voice.**

We do not have to be ordained ministers or high ranking officers of the church for God to transmit the ability to grasp His thoughts mentally and the willingness to tune in. His thoughts are objectively real, like electrical impulses or radio sound waves. When we gain knowledge to tune in there's no doubt of the authenticity of His presence, which will take us far beyond tranquil feelings to realize we have the confirmation of His existence. We have the certainty that we are not alone and that our behavior is being watched, but at the same time we experience a sense of tranquility and love. This is available to any Christian who desires the confirmation of the **Holy Trinity**.

Obtaining the providence and the grace of feeling God's presence takes effort just like anything else important in this life. When we spend time with the Lord and ask for the power of the Holy Spirit that abides in us. He will successfully lead us to the Son and then to the Father. We will find it profoundly meaningful and rewarding for our lives when we break the sound barrier and understand the vibrations of the Holy Spirit. Jesus said about the Holy Spirit,

"I will pray to the Father, and He will give you another Helper, that will abide with you forever." John 14:16

"I am the way, the truth, and the life. No one comes to the Father except through me." John 14:6

Religion is an institution established to teach belief in the divine power of the word of God. Each religion offers its own interpretations of scripture and what is expected of its membership. We humans are responsible for our own evolvement and acceleration of are own faith and spirituality. It will assist us in unlocking the secrets of a rewarding life. It is essential to belong to a church because spirituality is not just one person's active involvement. The activity must be exposed and shared. Jesus was not alone in His ministry, He had twelve disciples. Hopefully, the gifts of the Holy Spirit will invigorate our role in the church, exercising our faith in concert with others to praise the Lord. We the church are the body of Christ and our body is His temple; it all began after the ascension of Christ. God is the source of the church; Jesus is the head, and the Holy Spirit is the one that empowers the church.

"The Holy Ghost hath you overseers, to feed the church of God, which He had purchased with His own blood." Acts 20:28

"God promised those who asked will receive. Those who seek will find, those who knock will have doors opened to them." Matt. 7:7

God has endowed Anton's mind with private revelations through vibrations of the Holy Spirit for the quest of the divine. She will be sharing her story, addressing different subjects of her experience of searching for the integral part of the hidden message of the infinite mind of God.

* * *

In God we Trust

Oh, God please bestow blessings on our brothers and sisters. Give them a positive prescription for a meaningful spiritual Christian driven life and guide them to accomplish their mission. Help them hear Your voice through the Holy Spirit that patiently waits for the asking. Please God, bless them and their families and give them peace in their hearts. Grant them the wisdom and the knowledge to understand Your Son's word. Let them feel Your presence, oh God, we beseech you.

In the name of Your Son, Jesus Christ, we ask You to hear our prayers. We worship You, and humbly appreciate everything that you do for us. Let Your children drink of the living waters, so they will never thirst for anything more and let them feel Your unconditional love. Thank You.

Amen

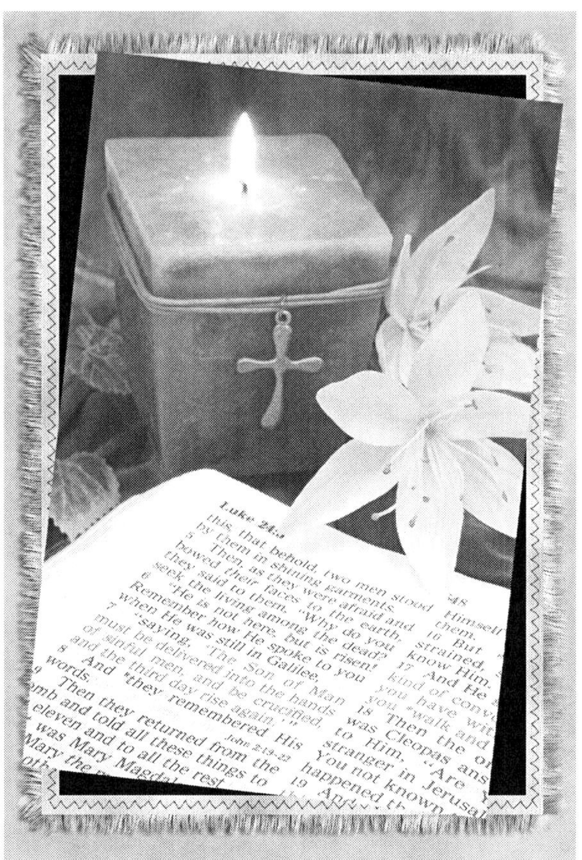

But I will sing of Your power; Yes, I will sing aloud of Your mercy I the morning; For You have been my defense And my refuge in the day of trouble. To You, O my strength, I will sing praises; For God is my defense, My God of mercy. Ps. 59:16-17

Chapter 1

BEARING WITNESS

Love and respect characterizes our attitude toward God and others.

"You are the light of the world. A city that is set on a hill cannot be hidden. Nor do they light a lamp and put it under a basket, but on a lampstand and gives light to all who are in the house." Matt. 5:14-15

By letting our light shine and convey our story, it may help somebody to have a deeper relationship with God. Sharing the uniqueness of our journey of faith and learning from each other will lead us to the main route and enlighten us with the major turning points of our path of life. We need each other for a fuller and more complete life.

Anton's manifestation of the Holy Spirit began one night while she was saying her prayers when the mystery occurred. All of a sudden there was a force of energy touching her head, moving it from left to right. She thought to herself, **"What in the world was that?"** It was not frightening, though; in fact, it was a pleasant feeling, like a tender loving touch. The movements went on for approximately the next five years before she let anyone know what was happening to her. This delay in questioning the movements went back to her discomfort about how sheltered her rearing was. She and her sister Lupe grew up in a rural area in Northern Mexico with their single working mother. When Anton was nine years old and her sister was eleven they were uprooted from their native country when their mother married a man who was a citizen of the United States. They immigrated to America and lived in El Paso, Texas. It was complicated living in a foreign city and not understanding the language people spoke. These were difficult times for the two sisters. The upbringing of children influences how they accept and perceive the experiences in their adult life.

"Beloved, do not believe every spirit, but test the spirits, whether they are of God." 1 John 4:1

Another reason for ignoring the manifestation was that Anton had heard Pastors say not to pay attention to physical feelings like goose bumps, tingling or even touching when they prayed. She figured her feelings should be strictly spiritual. In fact, a very popular and charismatic Pastor who admits God communicates with him, mentions in his preaching not to acknowledge any feelings of being touched that might go on while we pray. He should know that God is only trying to get our attention. This Pastor has wonderful information about scripture and God. He is anointed, (ordained by God) but it just shows us how even a man of God can have distorted image of God but still retain enough information to give him some important insights for his preaching. We are finite creatures, limited in how we perceive knowledge. An anointed person can sometimes be susceptible to error and not have the right interpretation or intention of the Lord. The recommendation is to always take the message into perspective. When in doubt we must use our own perception and ask the Holy Spirit for guidance to confirm scripture in the **Bible**.

The real truth of the matter lies in the fact that God is sometimes trying to attract our attention or to manifest His presence through the Holy Spirit, to insure us He does indeed exist and wants to make Himself known and show us that He is definitely with us. He might be trying to console us in time of distress or He has chosen us to accomplish a mission, even if we are not particularly seeking Him or whatever religious background we have. If God has chosen us for a particular reason or a task, private revelations will come without regarding our intellectual level. God will reveal Himself to the simple as well as the sophisticated. He knows we are all divinely equipped through His reflection; we are made in **God's image**.

GOD'S DISCLOSURE IS AN

EXPRESSION OF GRACE THROUGH NO

MERIT OF OUR OWN.

"God said; let them have dominion over all the earth." Genesis 1:26

We are God's hands and voice, plus we have dominion here on earth. This is precisely the reason that Jesus Christ had to be human also, besides divine. He had a mission to accomplish here on earth; He suffered the ultimate and died for our sins. This sacrificial act had to be consummated here on earth to be effective in the spiritual realm.

"His divine power has given to us all
things that pertain to life and godliness." 2 Peter 1:3

"Whatsoever thou shall bind on
earth shall be bound in heaven." Matt. 16:19

"I have come down from heaven, not to do
My own will, but the will of who sent Me." John 6:38

Anton finally got the nerve and the courage to ask someone about her experiences and she spoke to a clergyman. The clergyman stated, **"God is touching you."** He stated it so matter of factly that she found it hard to believe. We know about clergymen who claim to hear from God, which is hard to imagine. People who admit to possess a prophetic word are usually ridiculed. It is easy to understand why this woman kept the experience to herself for an additional five years. She surely did not want anybody making fun of her. She was curious though and determined to find out and discover the origin of where this force of energy that was touching her really came from. She came to the conclusion it had to come from the Lord; why would it manifest itself only when she prayed and why did she feel an enormous sense of love and security never experienced before? She finally found it very difficult not to react to this Mystic Person (The Holy Trinity) that is the Creator of our own lives. In fact, she found the experience to be very humbling, and she asked the Holy Spirit to guide her to do God's will. At this time she began studying the word of the Lord: the **Bible**.

THERE IS A BOND WITH

JESUS WHEN WE DO GOD'S WILL.

"Here are my mother and my brothers!
For whoever does the will of my Father in heaven
is my brother and sister and mother." Matt. 12:49-50

Anton's prayers initiated a blessing that empowered her with the sensitivity and wisdom of understanding the vibrations of the Holy Spirit. She actually understood what He was conveying. As this relationship evolves, our consciousness elevates to love, passion and ecstasy deep in our souls coming from a higher source with the ultimate expression of a caring divine heart that is from our Lord. Anton still did not tell anyone for a couple of years. She was afraid of exposing herself to criticism and of people thinking she was crazy or delusional, but after a while she became comfortable with the **experience**.

* * *

The reason for this information is to convince all Christians that have this same opportunity to not lose valuable time in trying to sort out this precious gift from God. She told her dear friend Pam and a few people in confidence. To her amazement and surprise, they were very kind with their responses, giving her confidence to become a witness for the Lord with her testimony. It is our duty as Christians to be witnesses to the Lord's word and presence, helping fuel and emphasize to believers the excitement and anticipation of having a dynamic correspondence through the Holy Spirit that will lead us successfully to the Father and Son, assuring us that we are not chasing an elusive dream and to have faith that we can step into a dimensional direction toward having communication with the Father. The Holy Spirit lives in the physical as well as in the spiritual realm. We can initiate and summon up the inner voice within us and ask God to give us supernatural confidence to believe that the Holy Spirit can be our friend as well as our Father. Our relationship with the Holy Spirit should not be considered differently from other relationships.

"It is to your advantage that I go away,
for if I do not go away, the Helper will not come to
you, but if I depart, I will send Him to you." John 16:7

The practical decision here is to never be negligent of God the Father's divine living presence. If we spend long periods in the presence of the Lord, meditating and studying the word, it will lead us to the power into the inner chamber within ourselves and fill us with the Holy Spirit. Our faith will increase by developing daily confidential conversation with our best Friend, strengthening our faith and giving us the authority of His existence in our lives. The purpose of this experience and journey is to be shared with one another, humbly giving our testimony of this spiritual knowledge if it is to remain **authentic**.

Our duty as Christians and spiritual mentors is to forge a transformation for those who are struggling with their spiritual guidance. There is a clear call for maturity in our spiritual adulthood walk. There is a process all believers have to experience in order to emerge a new creature in Christ and in this world. It is essential to understand there is a variation of one on one relationship with the Lord. All spiritual relationships are not equivalent. He knows we all perceive information differently; thus, He respects our independency and our unique structure. He will focus on our needs and He values the invitation into our lives and hearts. When we feel the presence of the Lord and understand the vibrations of the Holy Spirit, it is intriguing and fantastic to have this unique approach. Having communication with the unknown spiritual realm of Jesus Christ with the assistance of the Holy Spirit brings a dynamic value to our faith.

GOD IS NO RESPECTER OF PERSONS; WE ARE ALL THE SAME TO HIM.

I have become as a wonder to many, But You are my strong refuge. Let my mouth be filled with Your praise and with your glory all day. Psalm 71:7-8

This situation of having a Godly counsel has no time limits. The cultivation could take one day, a month, a year or longer. Mother Teresa of Calcutta kept a journal of her life where she wrote about her dry dark period of not feeling God's presence, but she knew deep in her soul that God was there. She knew if she persisted and stayed with the word that God would eventually lift that lonely dark time. She had extraordinary faith. She kept doing God's work in spite of this dryness. Mother Teresa's mission was caring for the poor. She felt a deep call to serve and love individuals who were sick and dying in Calcutta's ghettos, seeing Christ in the faces of the poor.

Telling the spiritual story of our circumstances that have been keys to our personal relationship with the Lord will help individuals with their journey. We all know there is a process of development to go through, and also acknowledge there are unique experiences according to the individual's family history. God considers circumstances, environment and the decisions we make according to our faith. He knows our complexity and what we are capable of doing, even when we feel an enormous emotional burden, because of what is expected of us. He will empower us to fulfill what we believe is an impossible task.

PSALM 19:1-6

The Perfect Revelation of the Lord

The heavens declare the glory of God; And the firmament shows His handiwork. Day unto day utters the speech, and night unto night reveals knowledge. There is no speech nor language where their voice is not heard. Their line has gone out through all the earth. And their words to the end of the world. In them He has set a tabernacle for the sun, which is like a bridegroom coming out of his chamber, and rejoices like a strong man to run its race. Its rising is from one end of heaven and its circuit to the other end, and there is nothing hidden from its heat.

The process here is to harbor, encourage, and affirm the existence of the Godly Counsel within us. We must assure believers that He will promote us when sufficiently ripe. That means when we are ready for a deep relationship with the Lord, knowing His mind and understanding His whispers through the vibrations of the Holy Spirit. Having this confirmation is worth praying frequently and becoming obedient to His authority through scripture. This gift and blessing comes with the responsibility of testifying of His divine living presence, through becoming witnesses to our testimony. He is alive just like He was two thousand years ago.

None of us can claim to possess the complete knowledge of God's creation. We are not psychologically, intellectually, or physically equipped to understand the mysteries and the whole evolution of the universe. But the wisdom and gifts the Holy Spirit has provided us with should be shared with one another, expressing our experiences of our spiritual dimensional gifts. These blessings are to equip us with the language of our spirit and to make a difference in people's lives. There are many Christians that are continually misinformed and naïve about the real concept of Christianity, as if it is a new religion. Our anxious heart is so preoccupied in search of happiness that we ignore our spirit's astute capacity to guide us to the impressive truth of happiness and the principal truth of the whole concept of God.

IS JESUS REALLY GOD? IS GOD REALLY

A LIVING GOD? HOW CAN THE TRINITY BE ONE?

HOW CAN THE HOLY SPIRIT BE JESUS AND GOD?

It is imperative to analyze the importance of our situation as Christians. Not being informed of this communication with the Holy Spirit impairs our growth and the wisdom we can acquire in our spiritual walk. It is beyond tragic to not believe that there is a conscious level where we reach spiritual maturity. Our faith began two thousand years ago. It is time for witnesses to stand together with their declaration and testify their unique and special relationship with the Father who will assist us in the present time.

That their hearts may be encouraged,
being knit together in love, and attaining to all
riches of the full assurance of the understanding, to the
knowledge of the mystery of God. Col. 2:2

GOD LIVES WITH US IN THE PRESENT TIME.

* * *

We are fallen creatures and need to be led, precisely the reason Jesus came to live among us. Our own life experience of faith can be examples, as icons to transform us into followers of Jesus Christ. In *Galatians 1:11* Paul's transformation was not immediate. In time he experienced a revelation of Jesus and he sought out understanding with other apostles to work out his calling and was passionate in his ministry. Having this communication with the Lord transcends us to another dimension; we are entering paradise. Reaching this level of consciousness and knowing with certainty the existence of God's realm, gives us the assurance we are walking in faith; it is as if God gives us glimpses of the eternal life. Walking in faith gives us a good relationship with God's children, making it a little easier to profess His word, which is every Christian's duty. The Bible commands us to be ministers of God's word. We all have the possibility and responsibility of instilling spiritual qualities and hope in our brothers and sisters. God wishes us to be in unity with each other in His Mystical Body.

In the New Testament the church (*ecclesia*) is a community

that has received the Holy Spirit and is now ready to do what is necessary to live out the gospel. It is the assembly of those who have become heirs of the promises of God; and because they have experience what that means for humanity, they cannot accept the world as it is.

James H. Cone

* * *

Anton was not approached until her early fifties. He knew she was not ready before to do her ministry until this period of her life. Now after all the physical and mental hurts of her life He has the affirmation of her maturity. He knew she was ready to bring this project into fruition. After many nights of soul searching she came to the conclusion that it was her duty to publish this message. She is not an authority in the field of theology, but for some extraordinary reason other than her love for the Lord, the Holy Spirit has placed in her heart the need to answer the calling of God. While she faced many obstacles in the past few years, her devotion was an overriding passion to honor Him and spread the news. With prayer, there is a possibility of the circulation of this message that will give us light in this time of chaos and darkness in the world, that we might see the spiritual road and be able to recognize and understand The Holy Spirit.

"I told them of the hand of my God which was good upon me. Then they set their hands to this good work." Neh. 2:18

"Do your little bit of good where you are; it's those little bits of good put together that overwhelm the world."

Archbishop Desmond Tutu

Anton's Background

Christian life can be simple; "take up the cross" maintain an inner quality knowing God is with us.

For we were saved in this hope, but hope that is seen is not hope; for why does one still hope for what he sees? Rom. 8:24

Maria Antonieta was born on August 26, 1944, in Chihuahua, Mexico in a village named Aldama. Her parents were Elena Beltran and Manuel Arzate. Elena had two girls when she lived in Mexico, Antonieta nicknamed Anton, Toni, and Toña and Guadalupe nicknamed Lupe who was two years older than Anton. The girls each had a different father which made their upbringing difficult. Elena was unable to remain faithful for any length of time in a relationship. She came from a dysfunctional family and was the oldest of five girls. When she was ten she suffered a horrific episode. Her father, in a drunken stupor, raped his oldest daughter. Since the incident occurred almost eighty years ago, nothing was done to help the child. The crime was never reported because people were afraid of this man. As a result of not receiving counseling, the terrible experience affected her entire life. It seemed like she lost part of her spirit. Although she remained a strong person, inwardly she became distant and cold. This feeling of indifference included her daughters. She was neglectful and careless. As a result these girls suffered all kinds of abuse. She was especially cold to Anton, because Elena was never in love with her father. He was much older than she, and it was a relationship of convenience which did not last long. She would say, **"I did not want this child. I never thought that old man would make me pregnant."** She said this like a joke, and Anton tried not to take it personally.

The Wicked Man

These six things the Lord hates, Yes seven are an abomination to Him: A proud look, a lying tongue, Hands that shed innocent blood, A heart that devises wicked plans, Feet that are swift in running to evil, A false witness who speaks lies, And one who sows discord among brethren. Prov. 6:16-19

Negative comments should never be said to a child even jokingly or in terms of endearment. If the child is sensitive and does not have a strong personality, such words will always haunt the child's life. The important element to consider is if our parents were abused, hurt or criticized as children. We must understand that where the negative comments are coming from has nothing to do with us. Maybe they were young and immature. Anton's best friend's father called her **"fatty"** when she was a child; the intent here was a love, pet name. But her friend said that she thought this affected her thinking as she grew up, because she felt she was supposed to be fat; she still has a weight problem. There's another possibility that she might have inherited a gene from the family. Perhaps we will never know. A single mother might be scared that she will not be able to provide for the baby. In an attempt to cover up her fear she will make negative comments. We must understand and recognize that our parents did not single us out to destroy our lives. Sometimes they are products of an unloving upbringing themselves. They are angry because they did not receive the attention and recognition they deserved as children. Their emotions are caused by what they are carrying in their hearts. When we comprehend these problems it will give us the ability to forgive them and forgive ourselves for condemning them, which in turn will open the door to the enlightenment of the Lord. Resentment will block God's grace in our lives to experience love and compassion. We understand that our life experiences shape us into who we are, and the lessons we learn show us how to behave and how to treat people. Hopefully, it will help us control our emotions to accept people as they are and realize that none of us are perfect. Acceptance of our past, that we did not have control of, will take us to a place free of resentments where we experience inner peace and closeness to the Lord with the ability to give love and receive **LOVE.**

* * *

I am not, then, the product of an assembly line. I am the carefully designed work of an artisan. I was conceived in eternity by love and I was born in time through Love. From the beginning and forever, I am freely loved by the Father.

Ignacio Larrañaga

It is amazing how people can live in poverty and survive, sometimes becoming stronger and even more grateful for everything as a result of the poverty of their childhood. Anton remembers the upbringing of the two girls and how difficult it was. When she was six years old and her older sister was eight, they and their mother were living in one room with four walls and a dirt floor. There was no running water or any indoor bathroom. They had to walk two miles every day to bring water to their little hovel. The water came from a single faucet that the government supplied to the rural areas of the city and which operated only half a day-in the morning. This water was for their every day use and to sprinkle on the dirt floor to keep the dust at a minimum. By then, they were living in Juarez, Chihuahua, Mexico.

Elena's four sisters would visit all the time and occasionally end up in cat fights. There was always some kind of turmoil going on in the family. Fortunately though, there was one good thing about them; they constantly talked about God, agreeing that He was our Father in heaven and would take care of us, love us, protect us and provide for us. They certainly did not want that horrible human being, their father, to be the real thing. They all resented him. Anton was a sensitive child and a profound thinker for as long as she can remember. When she heard that God was our Father that He loved us and was with us, she never felt alone. She talked to Him all the time and she remembers asking God, **"What were you thinking when you sent me to this**

crazy family?" She often wondered if it was not an imaginary figure that people had invented, even though she felt His presence. She also recalls even to this day, the time He demonstrated His existence and that He was hearing her. She was only eight years old when she decided to put God to a test. She was tired of being called (La negra) which means the dark one because the name hurt her feelings. She also knew the family was prejudiced against the darker tone. Every night she prayed, **"Please God make me lighter."** One day somebody mentioned, **"Have you all noticed that Toña is getting lighter?"** She was filled with happiness when she heard the comment, because it proved that He really did exist. Perhaps, God did not change the color of her skin, but He did change the way people perceived her. According to the vibrations of the Holy Spirit, she herself selected her color and race when she came into this world, so it makes more sense that He changed the way people perceived her. The main analogy here is that this incident gave her great faith, and now this little girl knew she had a protector she could depend on, and people started calling her by her name which is exactly what she wanted.

Who Is the Greatest?

At that time the disciples came to Jesus, saying, "Who is the greatest in the kingdom of heaven?" Then Jesus called a little child to him, set him in the midst of them, and said "Assuredly, I say to you, unless you are converted and become as a little children, you will by no means enter the kingdom of heaven. Therefore whoever humbles himself as this little child is the greatest in the kingdom of heaven. Whoever receives one little child like this in My name receives Me."
Matt.18:1-5

Often we do not recognize the answers to our prayers, because we are expecting immediate miracles. Not realizing that God's time is not the same as our time, most prayers are answered eventually as long as selfishness is not the purpose of our plea. Our job is to expect and recognize the answer, whether it takes one day, one month or years. When we align our will with God's will, our prayer can be very effective, not trying to control God, but letting Him direct us. Submitting our will is rarely uncomplicated; our humanism will experience some degree of struggle. Very often we will experience silence in an answer to our prayers, because we are lacking faith. If we expect answers to our prayers, we must completely rely on His wisdom and providence to answer. Recognizing answers to our prayers is to actually realize the way God's activity is trying to reach us. In fact, when we add **amen** to our prayers, we are actually thanking God for the expectancy of His answer, putting power to our petition.

"THY WILL, WILL BE DONE."

Reading the book THE FOUR AGREEMENTS by Don Miguel Ruiz with Janet Mills helped her realize God knew exactly what He was doing when He let Anton be in this family. Her childhood experiences seem to have purified her for adulthood. It has taught her not to be judgmental or take anything that happens personally. If we let bad circumstances affect us, we will be trapped in our own hell here on earth. She refuses to be offended by negative comments. We have to realize, that the perception of others is due to their own programming that they have allowed to perceive in their life. The realization and affirmation here is to be careful with whom we agree with. The point is, when we agree with somebody, we are agreeing with their assumption, their truth, their reality or their point of view. When we have this realization nothing can affect us or hurt us. If somebody says we are terrible or insults us we realize it is their own emotional baggage that they are carrying; we are immune to their beliefs. Unfortunately, not everybody is capable of learning from their misfortunes.

Anther lesson to learn is to never feel important, because this is the maximum expression of misguidance.

"God resists the proud, but gives grace to the humble." James 4:6

Trying to understand people's behavior and character can be very complicated. The important methodology to remember is the two greatest of all the commandments.

"You shall love the Lord your God with all your heart with all your soul, with all your mind and with all your strength. This is the first commandment." Mark 12:30

"The second, like it, is this: And you shall love your Neighbor as yourself. There is no other commandment greater than these." Mark 12:31

When people have been in the fire and purified, nobody can destroy their belief in being kind to others. Their emotions are intact, and they do not fear life or create an illusion of self importance. Love is still in their heart, even when they have to defend themselves and express their own point of view. (On the other hand, if some people claim that they are wonderful, they do not let this comment go to their head. It still is that person's own perception according to their own beliefs.)

HUMILITY IS HAPPINESS. WHEN

WE AGREE TO BE A SERVANT OF THE LORD

WE ARE AT PEACE, EVERYTHING IS WONDERFUL

AND IN A STATE OF BLISS. NOBODY CAN ROB US OF THE

JOY OF EXPERIENCING FREEDOM AND LOVE.

* * *

Anton does not feel qualified to give anybody advice. What is conveyed here is the information she has obtained from her subconscious mind by the grace of God, from some books and from the New King James Version Bible which has been used to help properly express her information. Dr. Joseph Murphy, D. R. S., PH.D.D. D., L.L.D., in a book The Power of Your Subconscious Mind, calls the subconscious mind **"The Treasure House Within You."** For example, being in harmony and tuning into our subconscious mind is very much like when people have reported near life/death experiences, and they reach a state of peacefulness. When we are alive and well and are able to tune into our subconscious mind, we reach a state of blissfulness difficult to be explained. It is so fantastic to acquire the Holy Spirit's knowledge that is in our subconscious, even though this information is frequently complicated to understand. It is a place where we accumulate our life experiences and God's information. This information is so awesome, because we seem to know how our loved ones are no matter in what part of the world they are in, because there is no time or space for our spirits. Of course, there are boundaries for this glorious gift, but our spirit seems to be aware of them and lets us know when we are acting inappropriately. We are actually tuning and tapping into the universal mind where we are all connected to make the **body of Christ.**

> *"That there should be no schism in the body, but that members should have the same care for one another. Now you are the body of Christ, and members individually." 1 Corinthians 12:25-27*

When Anton was eleven years old, her mother married Ray Carson. Surprisingly, the marriage lasted twenty-five years, until his death. Ray truly was Elena's soul mate. He was a good man. He literally adored her and did all he could to make her happy. Life changed dramatically for the entire family. Within one year, the decision was made for the whole family to move to the United States. Everyone was thrilled for the opportunity to start a new life. The family packed up their few belongings and entered the U.S. through the port of entry at El Paso, Texas. They came in on a green card, which is a permanent resident card, with the expectations that they would be working towards becoming naturalized citizens. They thought this experience in the U. S. was totally awesome even though they did not understand one word that was spoken to them. They loved having a television and watching the show, **"I Love Lucy."** Anton was intrigued and fascinated with the language. She wanted to learn English as fast as she could and comprehend what was going on with the characters on TV.

The move was done with high expectations. From the beginning everyone was hoping for a new life of happiness. Unfortunately, it did not last for long. The first serious problems to come up were with

Elena not wanting to stay home; many arguments began. Rather than trying to work out the problems, Elena would disappear almost on a daily basis.

Around 1959 Anton and Lupe welcomed a new sister Sylvia to the family, Thank God! She looked like her father! The family had been concerned about who the father might be and who the baby was going to look like. Ray's love might not have extended to a child that was not really his own now that they were married.

Life settled down for a while, but the girls had more responsibility with the birth of the new baby sister. The only positive thing was that Elena was staying home. Unfortunately, the constant fighting and bickering soon started again, like it had been before Sylvia was born. Anton could not stand it any longer. It was a very uncomfortable existence. Therefore, she dropped out of school.

Which none of the rulers of this age knew; for had they known, they would not have crucified the Lord of glory. But God has revealed them to us through His Spirit. For the Spirit searches all things, yes, the deep things of God. 1 Cor.2:8, 10

At sixteen she left home and went to work for an elderly lady as a companion. Now her existence was peaceful, indeed, to the point of boredom, just to sit around with this nice quiet lady who did not let her touch anything. This situation was more frustrating than all the commotion and turmoil she had at home. She never imagined that she would be grateful for her genes and family, but her life had transformed her into an active person, not negative, but active, with a strong personality like her mother. Thank God for her faith. She started praying for God to guide her to her next step. She read books, even the telephone book, to pass the time. She found several trade schools in the directory. She was able to save almost all of her salary, since she was living full-time with the lady. When she had enough money saved, she enrolled in Cosmetology School. Her mother promised to help her. Elena was basically a nice person; however, she let life and the world mold her instead of the Lord. God can use our life experiences to help and understand others. If we do not ask or allow God to help us, our misfortunes will hinder our evolution. Frequently, when Christians are partakers of Jesus' suffering and truly believe in His word with their heart He will reveal Himself to them, not when they are dead, but still alive in this world and they are walking in glory. When we hear or read that God will reveal Himself, we automatically assume that people are talking about when we die. This misconception must change with the testimony of witnesses.

"but rejoice to the extent that when you are partaker of Christ's sufferings, that when His glory is revealed, you may also be glad with exceeding joy." 1 Peter 4:13

Upon graduation, Anton honestly felt like Scarlett O'Hara in Gone With The Wind. She could take care of herself, and like Scarlett, she would never be **"hungry again."** Now armed with a vocation, she turned her training into a lucrative career. She never looked on those early days in a negative or hateful way. Instead, she thanked God for what she had to live through in order to give love, compassion and understanding for all kinds of people. When she started her adult life, she felt her penance and purity were over. It is not surprising that those who have exhibited some levels of holiness are usually those that have suffered the most. They give themselves to spiritual exercise and pursue service to humanity and to prayer.

"For he who has suffered in the flesh has ceased from sin, that he no longer should live the rest of the time in the flesh For the lust of men, but for the will of God." 1 Peter 4:1-2

Anton's concern is for teenagers, because she remembers how tremendously insecure and vulnerable she felt as a young adult. When young people have trouble at home or just have trouble growing up, they feel desolate. Because of their young nature some feel trapped and want their independence. They want to speed the process of growing up. This is a crucial age. Their hormones are changing and there is a transition taking place from child to adult. They need love, support, understanding and guidance. Some parents are so preoccupied with their own pressures and obligations that they fail to teach young people to exercise the limitations that are required in this world to grow up to be productive mature individuals and to live up to God's expectations for their lives. The nation's high school dropout rate is higher than we think; it is a **crisis.**

There was a special report by Nathan Thornburgh, "Dropout Nation" in TIME magazine, (April, 2006), p.31-35. It stated,

In today's data-happy era of accountability, testing and No Child Left behind, here is the most astonishing statistic in the whole field of education: an increasing number of researchers are saying that nearly 1 out of 3 public high school students won't graduate. For Latinos and African Americans, the rate approaches an alarming 50%. Virtually no community, small or large, rural or urban, has escaped the problem.

That's starting to change. During his most recent State of the Union address, President George W. Bush promised more resources to help children to stay in school, and democrats promptly attacked him for lacking a plan. The Bill and Melinda Gates Foundation has trained its moneyed eye on the problem by funding "The Silent Epidemic," a study issued in March that gained attention both in Washington and state houses around the country.

* * *

David's Song of Thanksgiving
Oh, give thanks to the Lord! Call upon His name; Make known His deeds among the peoples! Sing to Him, sing psalms to Him; Talk of all His wondrous works! Glory in His holy name; Let the hearts of those rejoice who seek the Lord! Seek the Lord and His strength; seek His face evermore! Remember His marvelous works which He has done.
1 Chr. 16:8-12

Anton is appreciative for her life and all her blessings, and she feels fortunate for the faith God has instilled in her heart all her life.

When we are lacking faith, some experiences are too overwhelming for us to handle alone. She realizes and admits how difficult life can become to cope with. Teenagers are especially close to her heart. She would like to reciprocate to God for all His blessings and be able to help the young people who have problems and help them focus on their purpose in life. This is the age of purpose, especially now with the popular book by Rick Warren, The Purpose Driven Life. When we learn and acknowledge our life's purpose that God has for us, then there is passion and enthusiasm for everything we do here on earth to accomplish our mission. Eighty percent of the proceeds from this book will go to help the young citizens of our nation. She also is grateful for this great country of ours and the opportunities it offers.

She has a wonderful career and is proprietor of her own businesses. She can testify that vocational careers bring success if a person is willing to work hard. Many times, a person with a vocational career can earn the same salary as a college graduate. An important statement that is essential to remember, is what John F. Kennedy said, **"It's not what your country can do for you, but what you can do for your country."**

"Anything you do for even the least of
my people here, you also did for me." Matt. 25:40

To continue with Anton's life story: she feels fortunate to have as her mate Jose Delgado. They have been married for forty four years. Her marriage was performed at a civil ceremony and made official with the church on their twenty fifth anniversary. It is constantly amazing to Anton that for the past forty four years her marriage has survived, especially with all the early frustrations, like the dysfunctional problems that she was able to leave behind. God's healing has allowed for her and her husband to always be able to work through the trials and tribulations of their married life.

She remembers when she first started to hear the Holy Spirit's vibrations that she felt she had to obey. When they were only going to attend a wedding reception, but, God wanted her to attend the church ceremony too. He wanted her to hear the Pastor who performed the ceremony say, **"If marriages stay close to the Lord, 85% will survive."**

MARRIAGE IS AN

INSTITUTION OF DIVINE ORDINANCE.

And the Lord God said, "It is not good that man should be alone: I will make him a helper comparable to him." Gen. 2:18

"Therefore a man shall leave his father and mother and be joined to his wife, and they shall become one flesh." Gen. 2:24

For as woman came from man, even so man also comes through woman; but all things are from God. 1 Cor. 11:12

The first year of Anton's marriage the couple welcomed their first child, Susana, into the family. Four years later Joe was born. Five years after, George entered the Delgado family. It has been a blessing that the ups and downs of a long-term marriage and raising her children with a life long commitment of love and responsibility have made her even more aware of the Lord's existence. Without His love and support the children would not be law abiding citizens with good moral values, and they are, Thanks to God! Now her inspiration is for all of them to be great Christians; one can only **hope and pray.**

That the sharing of your faith may become effective by the acknowledgment of every good thing which is in you in Christ Jesus. Therefore, though I might be very bold in Christ to command you what is fitting, yet for love's sake I rather appeal to you being such a one as Paul, the aged, and now a prisoner of Jesus Christ. Philem. 1:6, 8-9

Chapter 2

MANIFESTATION

Abide in mystery; God's infinite love, presence and action within us!

"If you abide in My word, you are My disciple indeed. And you shall know the truth, and the truth shall make you free." John 8:31-32

The majority of parents are so busy with hectic schedules of raising children and earning a living that they do not have much time left to spend with God or to have a relationship with Him. Of course, He hears their prayers and their requests when they need Him, even if they do not have a one-to-one relationship with him, for this process takes time and dedication. He understands their circumstances. Although, it is gratifying and wonderful to raise their children, it is still a struggle and a challenge. Because God makes us all unique, parents are constantly thinking of different ideas and tactics to deal with and help their children, just like He does. There is a purpose for the uniqueness of every child. They are all born with different talents to complete God's divine plan.

Let every soul be subject to the governing authorities.
For there is no authority except from God, and the authorities
that exist are appointed by God. Rom. 13:1

* * *

When Anton found herself with an empty nest, somebody mentioned to her that perhaps she had used her devotional faith as a crutch to survive her childhood. When we are not familiar with the word of the Lord, negative comments can shake our faith. She did wonder and rationalize, if she indeed had used her faith as an escape. Now she had time for deep thinking, just like when she was a child.

To achieve union with the Father and to direct our soul toward the infinite mystery of God, we need patience, love, hope and prayer for calmness and peace of mind, not letting interior distraction due to agitation and nervousness interrupt our concentration in our prayer. This is necessary in order for our prayer to be a bridge between our spirit and God's Spirit.

But the manifestation of the Spirit is
given to each one for the profit of all. 1 Cor. 12:7

Even though Anton, like so many people, had reservations about God's existence, she just felt better having faith and was more comfortable believing in the Almighty. Every night she would ask God for help, protection, guidance for her children, family, husband and herself, like many mothers do, and then she would pray the Lord's Prayer. Not really being religious, this was one of the few prayers she knew by heart. Have we noticed how strange our human disposition acts when we pray? We have all these petitions, because it's so natural for human beings to feel, **"What can you do for me?"** instead of asking, **"What can I do for you?"** **<u>The Lord's Prayer</u>** is a great petition prayer too, and a model prayer for believers to end the day and start the next day. We are asking for His blessings, **"Give us this day, our daily bread."** We are also asking for protection, **"Deliver us from evil."** Then we are asking for forgiveness, for we never know when our hour of death will be, so that we can join God in heaven. **"Forgive our trespasses as we forgive those who trespass against us."**

"For if you forgive men their trespasses, your
heavenly Father will also forgive you. But if you do not

forgive men their trespasses neither will your Father forgive your trespasses." Matt. 6:14-15

What she did not know was, **"Your kingdom come"** meant His second coming, but it also means asking for the Lord to bring His kingdom to live and reign in our hearts and in our lives.

The Lord's Prayer

Our Father who art in heaven, Hallowed be thy name. Your kingdom come. Thy will be done, on earth as it is in heaven. Give us this day our daily bread. And forgive us our trespasses, as we also forgive those who trespass against us. And lead us not into temptation, but deliver us from evil. For thy is the kingdom and the power and the glory forever, and ever Amen

* * *

The Lord's Prayer turn out to be a fantastic petition for Anton. After about a year of faithfully praying this prayer that Jesus gave us, the mystery was revealed like it was mentioned before. All of a sudden, one night when she was praying, an unforeseen gentle force, like a sneak attack, touched her head on the left side. She could feel the Lord's powerful presence, confirming her faith and shaking the core of her being forever. All this happened by pure coincidence and accidentally because she did not know she was meditating on the Word, since she was not familiar with the Bible and not concerned with anything spiritual. She just tried to live with faith, but this faith helped her discover a wonderful gift. Now she had to learn a different type of schooling, especially psychological and spiritual educational laws. She questioned this spectacular, spontaneous event and wondered, "**Why me?"** But the primary reality is that God is free and we cannot question His actions or we will end up in complete confusion, because we must realize God is in different orbits. The philosophy to learn is that God cannot be reached without effort, order, and methods.

"Eyes have not seen, nor ear heard, nor have entered into the heart of man the things which God has prepared for those who love Him." 1 Cor. 2:9

Anton's constant praying had helped her reach contemplation, which is a way of making ourselves aware of God's presence, one remains in mystery, which means to visualize being in His presence. The physical touch from the Holy Spirit was the first stage of this particular experience. He was demonstrating His presence before any other disclosure would take place. There's a process we all have to go through when starting a relationship, especially with the Father that we have heard and read about, but we have never actually been involved with. Hearing about the qualifications of the Father is no substitute for the real-life experience of knowing Him. We are acquiring knowledge through the senses and not through abstract reasoning. We must try to be receptive and to keep an open mind about contemplation in order to let His intellect come through and allow the revelation of Himself to proceed. With prayer and patience all things are possible. His presence will emerge in amazement and glory to the individual who is seeking Him. This disclosure can ultimately be simple, but we frequently find it difficult to trust that such a simple revelation is happening. God revealed Himself to Moses in the burning bush when he asked,

"Please, show me Your Glory?" But He said, "You cannot see My face; for no man shall see Me, and live." Ex. 33:18, 20

Job heard God's voice from out of the whirlwind.

The Lord Reveals His Omnipotence to Job 38:1

For some unexplained reason, we are so skeptical in this time. We feel these aforementioned issues that occurred over 2,000 years ago can no longer happen in our modern times. This is precisely the reason why witnesses should have the courage to accept the responsibility to testify to the reality and to the authenticity of these passages that are quoted in the Bible. They are realistic examples of acknowledgment of how God identifies Himself to human beings.

"Be still, and know that I am God; I will be exalted among the nations, I will be exalted in the earth!" Psalm 46:10

* * *

Meditating and quieting our mind will transcend us to the dimension where we can experience a meaningful relationship with the Lord. This communion will activate a significant doctrine leading us to the understanding of the passion God has for our lives. We need to evoke this passion with patience and an appetite for the truth of His existence. Maintaining the activity of this relationship will impart us with special support and power; it will deliver us to the instinct of submission and surrender. God has distinct avenues of revealing Himself to a person's understanding of His presence. He grants all of us different gifts to be able to compliment each other with His grace for the whole comprehension of His divine purpose, but obtaining these special gifts is complicated for us busy and preoccupied mortals. We need to find and search ways to concentrate on a state of relaxation of our mind to lead us to produce meditation which will enable us with the inclination to the first step to the enlightenment of contemplation.

This psychological experience will take the individual to different higher advanced levels of consciousness. This extraordinary process will slowly and gradually transcend us to a region of peace, strength and joy, automatically maintaining God as the center of our life, and feeling different sensations and emotions with the realization that God is not to be feared or inaccessible. This relationship will equip us with spiritual truth and self knowledge. We will be capable of transcending to a higher level of awareness. It will blossom to inner peace and to the comprehension and conformity of our selves and of our lives. The beauty and astonishment of this state of consciousness is to develop the ability of knowing the confusing truth of God's mind. We need to equip ourselves with His wisdom in order to discover the whole truth of the infinity of God's purpose.

* * *

THE SECRET TO SUCCESS IS PERSEVERANCE

IN THE PHYSICAL AS WELL AS IN THE SPIRITUAL.

"This is the word of the Lord to Zerubbabel: not by might, but by My Spirit, Says the Lord of hosts. Zech. 4:6

In order to reach this introspective encounter that is a meeting of two entities forming an element of one, we need to master and exercise the skill to dominate and control our human mind that is constantly thinking of the past, the present and the future. To wander is one of the characteristic natures of the mind which is constantly in perpetual motion. It is difficult for us to concentrate on just the present time, which is when God is with us. Overcoming distractions seems impossible sometimes. Starting this proposition can be frustrating at times, for it takes concentration on disengaging ourselves from our preoccupations and worries that we harbor in our mind which destroy our peace and calmness. The active person is always busy thinking and planning ambitious projects and the worrier wrestles with psychological problems. Our world is so complex, that our mind goes off in uncontrollable directions. And then there are illnesses we also have to endure. All these difficulties and distractions make it impossible to control the inner peace of our mind. But if we try to meditate frequently, we will succeed; it's like children trying to walk. **"Practice makes the master."** With patience and a real desire of mastering meditation, we will achieve this process to start our **encounter.**

IF GOD HAS GIVEN US SPIRITUAL

INSIGHTS, WE MUST USE THEM FOR HIS

SERVICE REGARDLESS OF OUR AGE.

"And other sheep I have which are not of this fold,

them also I must bring, and they will hear "My voice;" and there should be one flock and one shepherd. John 10:16

Ask God to guide us to discover what will help us to facilitate this state of mind. Disengage ourselves from preoccupation and quiet our mind. It could be as simple as walking, swimming, running and praying, whatever method that works to silence the noise of the interior of our conscious mind. Our subconscious mind is already quiet. This is precisely where we need to arrive, where our spirit and the Holy Spirit **coexists.**

Praying meditatively can even be reached by repeating **"amen."** It may help induce this fundamental meditative state, moving beyond words. For Billy Graham, **"The first step in prayer is to choose a proper setting: a quiet spot where you won't be disturbed while you seek to be alone with God; next, ridding your mind of anger or animosity and engaging the Lord in one-on-one conversation."**

* * *

There is a little book that explains meditation adequately. It is written by Patrick Wanis and its title is <u>Finding GOD Spiritual Strategies to Help YOU Find Happiness, Fulfillment and Inner Peace.</u> The author, a human behavior expert reveals how connecting with the higher power can help us create a happier and healthier life. The book states,

Almost all of the spiritual masters and great teachers set aside time for meditation, a powerful way to achieve love, peace and self-acceptance. Meditation is a way to stop those loud racing, endless thoughts, doubts and distractions that come from our rushed, stressed world and our attachment to material things. Meditation helps us access the right hemisphere of the brain, the seat of intuition and creativity. Through the right side of the brain and meditation we can focus on beauty, spirituality and divine inspiration, searching for peace in a troubled world.

* * *

There was an article by Meg Grant in the Reader's Digest, December 2006, The article tells about Will Smith and is entitled "Why He Can't Stop Running." When he was asked if he has always been a runner, this was his response,

I started about five years ago. Running introduces you to your worst enemy, to that person who tells you, "Ooh, our ankles hurt and we should stop. Why do we need to run five miles? Let us do three." That is the same person who says to a man, "Hey, your wife will never find out if you sleep with her," and the same person who tells the 16-year old, "You are not gonna be cool if you do not smoke it." If you start giving in to that person, you will never get to your goals.

* * *

ANY METHOD THAT CAN HELP US TO

MEDITATE, WILL HELP US DISCERN BETWEEN

WHAT IS GOOD AND WHAT IS BAD.

Meditation often causes illumination. It will bring understanding to circumstances that are difficult to comprehend. The Holy Spirit will give us the confirmation of doubts we might have about any given situation, through vibrations or other means that He can present to us. He will settle any suspicions we might have of what is right or wrong about any situation or problem that we are faced with. God makes certain, that we get answers if we are seeking Him, but sometimes we don't realize or recognize His assistance

In manifestation we learn to listen to the Lord, but first we need to arrive at the secret corner of our soul, isolating ourselves from distractions that overwhelm our existence. We must also surrender ourselves to the quietness of the Lord. It is essential to reach that bridge where the encounter (interior unity) will occur, touching each other spiritually. This unfathomable mystery will start a process of communing with the Lord. The process will be slow and gradual. Incorporating our life with His will take time. It is difficult and complicated for human beings to give up our independence, because God equipped us with free will. We need to do battle with these evolutionary laws of our lives. We go through purification and detachment of ourselves to proceed with God's direction to the architecture of the transformation of truly becoming a **"child of God,"** a living image of His Son Jesus Christ transcending us to a region of peace, strength and joy. This is an ecstasy of happiness too complicated and difficult to fathom, reaching higher levels where we experience supernatural, psychological and special support for our **life**.

WE NEED TO BE PATIENT

TO PRODUCE PERSERVERANCE,

KEEP SEEKING AND ASKING.

"I say to you, though he will not rise and give to him because he is his friend, yet because of his persistence he will rise and give him as he needs. For everyone who asks receives, and he who seeks finds and to him who knocks it will be opened." Luke 11:8, 10

* * *

In order to travel this journey to the kingdom of God, we must be determined to reach this state of consciousness and meditation to start our dialogue with the Lord. There's a series of interpersonal dynamics we experience for the foundation and involvement of this encounter. The Lord wants us to increase our knowledge of Himself in order to obtain this familiarity of His Spirit. There are emotions to contend with too; we wonder if we are intellectually and emotionally stable. We feel that we are imagining this phenomenal experience of having this type of communication. The alternative here is we need to do our research on the Lord through scripture in the Bible. That is the reason for steps to this unity, where there are no leaps. It is because God considers our human nature and waits for the steps to be in accordance to our intellect.

Our petition prayers need to go through a formation and manufacture in the spiritual realm before they materialize in the physical. Therefore, our imagination is extremely important when we pray. This is the motive for saying **"amen"** (praising the Lord and agreeing on the request) at the end of a prayer. We are imagining that our petition has already materialized and has taken place, and we are thanking the Lord.

IN ORDER FOR MEDITATION TO

TRANSCEND US TO CONTEMPLATION

WE MUST IMAGINE THE LORD IS WITH US.

The definition of contemplation; Editor in Chief, Sidney I. Landau, The New International Webster's Dictionary Thesaurus Atlas.

Con-tem-plate, 1 To look at attentively, 2 To consider thoughtfully; ponder, 3 to intend or plan, 4 to treat as possible.

* * *

It is recommended to start a vocal prayer, spiritual reading and studying the Bible. We should find a place where we can be alone and concentrate on our prayer. Now we need to focus on breathing deep and freeing our mind of any concerns that can disturb our concentration, thinking in the moment and filling ourselves with love for everybody. Try to eliminate any resentment we might have stored in our heart. This action should allow us to reach a conscious state of relaxation, with no worries, just like when we were babies. Pretend we are in the arms of the Father where nothing can affect us or hurt us.

Now is the time for gratitude which will empower us with qualities and instincts. We could say **"thank you God"** several times or other similar phrases that will help us into a state of meditation, letting our awareness of time disappear and letting our mind go blank. Creating an interior emptiness, to the point where consciousness is made complete; (awareness of God) entire being is silence. The mind retains absolute control over itself, integrating everything in the present time. This is how we attain a total grand **spiritual experience**.

But you are not in the flesh but in the Spirit, if
indeed the Spirit of God dwells in you. Now if anyone does
not have the Spirit of Christ, he is not His. For you did not receive
the spirit of bondage again to fear, but you received the spirit of adoption
by whom we cry out, "Abba, Father."
Rom. 8:9, 15

There are other procedures or activities that will bring peace of mind and reconciliation with the Lord, producing a state of meditation. For example, being alone with nature has the tendency of calming anxieties and nervousness with the inclination of being aware and concentrating on the Creator. After we accomplish the art of meditation, it won't be necessary to be alone. We can will ourselves into this state of meditation anywhere at any time because we have learned to quiet our mind even if noise surrounds us. Mastering this action of meditation produces an overall wellness to our health. It enhances our immune system by lessening anxiety and depression, which in turn will reduce our production of stress hormones. It could lower heart rate and high blood pressure.

Peace is not merely a distant goal that
we seek, but a way by which we arrive at our goal.

Martin Luther King

Contemplation

We marvel in the fact that God is willing to live in sinful people. In return, all He expects is for us to get to know Him.

"I will dwell in them and walk among them. I will be their God, and they shall be My people. I will be a Father to you, and you shall be My sons and daughters, says the Lord Almighty." 2 Cor. 6:16, 18

Anton finds herself with this evidence and demonstration of the sureness of the reality of the spiritual realm. This interaction of the state of contemplation made her content and appreciative. She now had the realization and confirmation with the manifestation of the Spirit that was touching her that we are not alone in this world, but she still remained naïve to the whole nature of the situation. She did not realize there was another step that was even greater than contemplation, which is **revelation.**

God shows His presence as gentle, quiet and loving, but still remains obscure His presence is scattered and indirect. He does not want to interfere with our independence, free will, our learning process and our evolution. For this reason, He waits patiently for the acceptance of His invitation for our acquaintance. He will respect those that resist and refuse **His company.**

* * *

The Prodigal Son: A Bible story about a father with two sons, who gives the youngest son part of the family estate at his request.

And not many days after, the younger son gathered all together, journeyed to a far country, and there wasted his possessions with prodigal living. Luke 15:13

When the youngest son found himself destitute, he went home. His father received him with open arms and gave a party in his honor. The oldest son feels unappreciated and pouts. His father patiently pleads with him to understand the situation.

* * *

God's divine nature is gracious and generous without being selective or making exceptions of His love for His children. He loves us all, for His love is unmerited and indiscriminative.

Who shall separate us from the love of Christ? Shall tribulation, or distress, or persecution, or peril? Nor heights nor depths, nor any other created thing, shall be able to separate us from the love of God. Rom. 8:35, 39

We adults are like children, experiencing circumstances and still learning about life with bits of illumination from the Father who waits patiently for our recognition and response.

The first thought that comes to mind, when we discover and learn about these fundamental steps of meditation, contemplation and revelation is how come we are not informed by our parishioners about how important this information is, in order to have a relationship with the Lord. The profound expression of contemplation and revelation is a union with God that we might become one. Jesus said,

"And the glory which You gave Me I have given them, that they may be one just as We are one." John 17:22

WHEN WE HAVE THE ASSURANCE OF THE

PRESENCE OF GOD WE CAN HANDLE ANY TEST.

For in the time of trouble He shall hide me in His pavilion; In the secret place of His tabernacle He shall hide me; He shall set me high upon a rock. Psalm 27:5

Some clergy of all religions have the assumption that their parishes are not prepared to hear that God actually talks to people. The clergy is doing us all disservice by keeping us uninformed of this communication, because nobody actually knows when the Lord will choose to have a personal relationship with a person. Keeping us ignorant of this supernatural fact truly leaves us unprepared for such an unnerving powerful experience. We do not know what is happening or what to make of this interior force that unexpectedly becomes activated; which is the Holy Spirit. We should be prepared for this magnificent possibility and not waste time trying to unravel the activity and start to live this wonderful experience that will change our lives.

* * *

Peter, the disciple of Jesus, completely changed when the Holy Spirit descended upon him at the ascension of Jesus; he was transformed. Peter had several conflicting qualities. He was energetic, self-confident and daring, but he also was unstable, weak and cowardly. The transformation made him stable, humble and courageous for the service of the Lord; he became a noble pillar of the church. This was a special meaningful event that took place at the ascension of Jesus. All present received the Holy Spirit, and it was activated immediately.

"And suddenly there came a sound from heaven, as of a rushing mighty wind, and it filled the whole house where they were sitting. Then there appeared to them divided tongues, as of fire, and one sat upon each of them. Acts 2:2-3

Looking at the other side of the equation, clergymen do not teach us all we need to know about Christianity. They probably think that there is a large degree of understanding and learning of important concepts from the Bible, which also may be confusing and complicated.

It would be impossible for the clergy to teach us theology and, at the same time, teach us how to have a deep meaningful relationship with the Lord. Their job is to manufacture Christians; to help us understand the whole design of the theology of the life of Jesus and the trinity. Their hope is that through their teaching it will help us with our everyday lives and save souls through the word of the Lord. Perhaps, it should be our interest and duty to search for different avenues to get close to the Lord once we learn of His word and His existence. It is time we think more incisively about the nature of contemplative prayer. It is a problem that most of us do not realize that everyone has the ability and the capacity to have a relationship with the Lord; it is not beyond us or just reserved for only a few.

Martin Luther vigorously insisted that our Search for God would be futile if it were not for God's own willingness to reveal Himself.

God is searching for children with loving natures, even if they are ignorant about His written word. For His powers show better in uninformed human creatures, because their intellect will not blind them to the information. Anton would pray to God; it was simpler and easier. Why get involved in scripture? She loved Jesus, but never directed her prayers to Him and ignored the Holy Spirit completely. Like so many misguided Christians, she did not bother with anybody else. She just went to the source--the Almighty, forgetting the one that converted us and made us the children of God. This is a common misconception. We don't realize that if it was not for Jesus, we Gentiles would not be included as children of the real God. Jesus gave us the right and the privilege of the initiation into the family of God by being adopted through baptism and accepting Jesus as our Lord and savior. We are born again through the Spirit and have the opportunity of eternal life. Jesus said,

"Most assuredly, I say to you, unless one is born of water and the Spirit, he cannot enter the kingdom of God." John 3:5

The subject of belief can easily lose the attention of the misinformed and it can lose its place in the realm of thoughtful truth, the real truth of Jesus Christ. Learning and believing the word of the Lord will assist us in this complicated world. It is unfortunate not to be informed about the complete message or on getting our facts together on the subject of Jesus' life. We also should be able to relate our circumstances in our lives to His life. It is important and necessary for our hopes, intentions and inspirations that we might have for our life. Only when we confront our own mystery, can we know the fundamental reason for our existence.

IF WE TRY TO KNOW THE LORD,

HE WILL REVEAL HIMSELF AND WE WILL

KNOW THE TRUTH OF OUR EXISTENCE.

"Everyone who is of the truth hears My voice." John 18:37

We human beings can experience confusion about our origins. We have the tendency to forget our capability through the likeness of God's image and being in His image. We are inclined to ignore our potential and the capability of achieving the impossible. We seem, by nature, to limit ourselves through our perils without realizing our qualities and not letting them evolve and develop to their full potential. God's glory was wonderful in the structure of humankind and all the virtues He has bestowed on us since the beginning of time.

* * *

Time goes on; approximately seven years have gone by in Anton's life since she felt the first manifestation of the force that touched the left side of her head when she prayed. She was so used to the touch that it became second nature to her. Now that she could look back at the circumstances, she wondered if somebody would have prepared her for this manifestation that perhaps it would not have taken her all these years to recognize the Holy Spirit was trying to get her attention.

She feels she wasted valuable time making this magnificent discovery that God is not One that alienates Himself after we are born. He does not cut the umbilical cord and leave us all alone with the struggles and tribulations of life.

A person can become accustomed to a mystical touch, but it cannot be easily ignored for this touch produces an ecstatic, delightful and intense emotion that comes with the awareness of actually feeling the powerful presence of the Lord. The Bible says this about **Jesus**,

And for this reason He is the Mediator of the new covenant, by means of death, for the redemption of the transgressions under the first covenant, that those who are called may receive the promise of the eternal inheritance. Heb. 9:15

* * *

All Anton thought was that this manifestation was of God, but she had no idea what it really was. One night, for some unexplained reason, when she was saying her prayers she decided to ask, whatever was touching her, **"Are you a spirit and would you like to communicate with me?"** For the first time, the touch was not moving her head from left to right, but the touch came under her chin, forcing her head to move from up to down. She realized it was being moved to nod a **"yes."** It really shocked her. She thought, **"Oh my God, this energy is alive!"** But by now she knew enough spiritual theology to know it was a good spirit. She could not believe she was not fearful and felt calm, for she felt protected. According to every day life this should not be happening. She thought, **"This is like being in a fictional movie."** She was a little apprehensive, but determined to continue with this conversation. The first question she asked was, **"Who are you?"** No answer was received. Her ears were not sensitive to the vibrations yet, even though she was sensitive to the touch and His presence. There is a process for everything; God has to prepare the ground first. The dialogue was **"yes"** and **"no"** to begin with. Having a firm belief in angels, she thought that was whom she was communicating with. Eventually, she could hear words without sound, like mental telepathy.

Finally, one night she heard the explanation of what the action of this touching was. She was being contacted directly by the Holy Spirit. She spoke out loud for confirmation by asking if indeed it was the Holy Spirit. Her head shook and nodded a **"yes."**

American theologian, Reinhold Niebuhr,
describes the grace of general revelation in this way,
"Private revelation is the testimony in the consciousness of every person that his life touches a reality beyond himself, a reality deeper and higher than the system of nature in which he stands."

This mystical event of revelation will revolutionize our life with the acceptance of Christ's invitation to follow Him in the journey of spiritual life. When the Holy Spirit is active in our lives we also attain His fruits which are love, joy, peace, patience, kindness and goodness. We might also be given some of the gifts of the Holy Spirit which the apostle **Paul lists in,** *1 Corinthians 12:9*

1-*The word of wisdom,*

2-*The word of knowledge,*

3-*Faith,*

4-*Gifts of healing,*

5-*The work of miracles,*

6-*Prophecy,*

7-*Discerning of spirits,*

8-*Different kinds of tongues,*

9-*Interpretations of tongues.*

The Holy Spirit gifts are given according to the sovereign of the Holy Spirit. Each of us has a unique combination of personality traits. All this is taken into consideration as we receive our spiritual gifts to use in our work for the Lord. All members have different abilities. It is improper to expect everyone to function well in all areas. God has given us all different abilities, concerns, insights and interests. He did not intend for all to have the same talents and tasks. Each has a duty to God to pursue his or her own gifts for His glory.

* * *

This adventure of being friends with the father will transform us into devoted witnesses of His existence with the obligation of annunciating and proclaiming the Son's living image. Because of the realization and the confirmation of God's existence, prayer takes on a whole different dimension; an appreciation of the value of prayer grows and we become more aware that it is actually a dialogue with the father. We can call for His strength, assistance and understanding of our every day problems, thus widening the horizon.

Revelation is not the transmission of a body of knowledge, but the personal disclosure of one subject to other subjects. God has taken the initiative and has freely made known the divine identity and purpose.

Daniel L. Migliore

When we experience revelation from the spiritual realm, we can truly relate and understand Jesus Christ throughout His life with us. Even though He was on earth, He remained in communion with the Father. When the Holy Spirit descended upon Jesus, they became One, establishing the bond for the **Holy Trinity.** This happened when Jesus was baptized. John the Baptist did not think he should baptize Jesus, but Jesus knew it was the proper thing to do.

*And John tried to prevent Him, saying,
"I need to be baptized by you, and are you coming to
me?" "Permit it to be so now, for thus it is fitting
for us to fulfill all righteousness."* Matt. 3:14-15

*"I have come, not to do my own will,
but the will of Him who sent me."* John 6:38

*"My Father, if it is possible, let this cup pass from
me; yet not what I want, but what you want."* Matt. 26:39

* * *

Duty: As believers and children of the true God we must do what is proper to do, which is spread the Gospel. When we are baptized one of our duties is to become ministers of God's word.

In the Old Testament Esther knew what her duty was. Her story is one of the most exciting books in the Old Testament. It tells of a Jewish orphan girl who, by her beauty and courage, saved her people from extermination. No one in Persia knew of Esther's heritage. The king discovered her, when in search for a new queen, because the old one enraged him by defying him. King Xerxes married Esther because he was overwhelmed by her beauty. After a while, one of the king's officials was furious at Esther's cousin Mordecai. The official convinced the king to sign an order to exterminate all the Jews in Persia. Mordecai sent a message to Esther, urging her to intercede for the good of her people. Esther knew the ways of the court. She knew the penalty for tampering with the affairs of the court was death. She reminded Mordecai of what could happen. When Mordecai heard the response, he sent her a note.

*Do not think that in the king's palace you will escape any
more than all the other Jews. For if you keep silence at such a
time as this, relief and deliverance will rise for the Jews from
anther quarter, but you and your father's family will perish.
Who knows? Perhaps you have come to royal dignity for just*

such a time as this. Esth. 4:13-14

The note touched Esther's heart. This is what happens when we hear a prophetic word. She knew it was a call from God. After all, she was one of God's own people. Remembering her identity gave her power, strength and courage. Perhaps Mordecai was right. This was precisely the reason for her elevated royal position in her life. God will not ask us to do anything without empowering us first with the necessary equipment. Esther sent word to her cousin Mordecai.

"Go, gather all the Jews to be found in Shushan, and hold a fast on my behalf. I and my maids will also fast as you do. After that I will go to the king, though it is against the law; and if I perish, I perish." Esth. 4:16

Risking her life, Esther went before the king. He received her favorably, lifted the edict, and elevated the status of all the Jews in Persia.

THIS IS AN EXAMPLE OF WHAT IT MEANS TO

BE A CHILD OF GOD; COMPLETE ABANDONMENT

TO THE CARE OF THE LORD.

* * *

A Christian is a perfectly free lord of all, and a subject to no one. A Christian is a perfectly dutiful servant of all, subject to all.

Gregory of Nyssa

When I remember You on my bed, I meditate on You in the nigh watches. Because You have been my help, Therefore in the shadow of Your wings I will rejoice. My soul follows close behind You; Your right hand upholds me. Ps. 63:6-8

Revelation

The Holy Spirit exercises the power of the Father and Son. He is commissioned to speak in their name.

"But when the Helper comes, whom I shall send to you from the Father, the Spirit of the truth who proceeds from the Father, He will testify of Me." John 15:26

Anton was amazed and intrigued with her mysterious encounter with the Holy Spirit. She looked forward to her evening prayers before going to sleep. It was fascinating asking questions about all the things she ever wondered about or doubted. The first major question was, **"What is your role in the Holy Trinity?"** We all know that God is the Father and Jesus is the Son, but some Christians often question the purpose of the Holy Spirit in the Holy Trinity. She hoped that she was not offending Him. After all, He is referred to as God, the Holy Spirit. But, she truly wanted to know the explanation of anything He would be willing to tell her. The Holy Spirit's vibrations explained the answer to her question in a manner that she would understand. He did not use esoteric theology or deep explanation that would take years of study to unravel. He took her simple question and answered it in a simple manner, just like we all need to hear. The Holy Spirit's vibrations explained, **"I am a Spirit and I am the connection between the Father and the Son, which when connected, makes us three in one."** He also explained, **"I am all of humanity's connection to God's kingdom."** The fundamental and profound explanation of the mystery of the Holy Spirit is that we all have a connection to all three and can contact any of them at any time.

AFTER JESUS ASCENDED TO HEAVEN,

HE SENT HIS PRESENCE TO ALL BELIEVERS

THROUGH THE HOLY SPIRIT.

The Bible, speaking to us and heard by us as God's Word, bears witness to past revelation. Proclamation, speaking to us and heard by us as God's Word, promises future revelation.

Karl Barth

The Holy Spirit has begun a broader work with humanity. The essence of his doctrine carries the authority of God, just as it has for centuries. We human beings seem to complicate beliefs and truths of knowledgeable stories in the Bible. The independent way, is to realize the truth of the Lord is not an activity of intellectual understanding, but of the heart where the Holy Spirit resides. He will give us the knowledge and the exegetical clarity of the peaks of theology. The more we submerge ourselves in the depths of the Holy Spirit, the brighter the light in our mind by possessing the Divine Essence of the Lord. We will soar to the highest heights of understanding of the truth, with new eyes of faith, similar to the eyes of the body through which we see material things. But, through spiritual eyes we can experience the doctrine of the Holy Trinity and have a relationship with the Lord.

In the Old Testament the Lord God promised to give a new heart to God's people and put His Spirit within them.

"I will put my Spirit within you and cause you to walk in My statutes. I will deliver you from all your uncleannesses."
Ezek. 36:27, 29

The truth that God is God and our Lord, and further truth that we could know Him as God and Lord, can only come to us through the truth itself. This *"coming to us"* of the truth is revelation.

Karl Barth

* * *

When a person reaches the level of private revelation, the first impulse and desire is to be a witness and share this fantastic privilege that God has bestowed on us, to actually be able to communicate with the Holy Spirit. The enthusiasm that we feel is too complicated to explain, because it seems a veil is removed from our eyes and we see the truth of life, understanding the celebrations and tribulations of life; the ups and downs. We do not have to ask ourselves why does God do this or why does He allow this? Tapping into the universal mind of God, gives us the understanding of the evolution of life, acquiring the ability to grasp the meaning to perceive and explain the significance of circumstances. We are being sanctified, (a source of grace) a blessing to higher status, while we are still in this difficult world. We are having fellowship with the Lord when it can be essential to our existence. Of course, it is wonderful as Christians to know that we have the opportunity to be saved when we die. But, this seems to be so distant, because we all expect to live for many years. The fact stands, that with this friendship we are never alone. He will help us with simple decisions, as well as with important ones that we face every day if we ask for His assistance. The misconception that most people have is that we should not bother God with simple and insignificant problems. But just the fact that we are acknowledging and recognizing His existence, even with simple decisions, is a form of worship. Comprehending God's love that He has for humans will give us the knowledge to understand why worshiping is so important to Him, because His ultimate burning desire is for us to join Him in heaven when we die.

For the Scripture says, "Whoever believes on Him will not be put to shame." For "Whoever calls on the name of the Lord shall be saved." Rom. 10:11, 13

WORSHIP IS TO ACKNOWLEDGE GOD'S

PRESENCE, THAT IS DIVINE, SHOWING RESPECT,

DEVOTION AND ADMIRATION OF HIS GREAT WORTH.

The problem with humans about the subject of heaven is that we want to attain our rewards now; we are a now generation. Someone described Americans as people who want to go to heaven without having to die, and, in a way, that person is correct. This is precisely the reason for this information. When we have a friendship with the Father, we feel we are in heaven. We are not from this world any more. We walk in faith and glory and awareness of the supernatural happenings around us. Nothing can affect us, not even death, because we do not exist under the law of the world and are not afraid to die. If we lose loved ones, we have the confirmation that they are going to a better place, which is a tremendous satisfaction for the one left behind.

But, if you are led by the Spirit, you are not under the law. Gal. 5:18

But now we have been delivered from the law, having died to what we were held by, so that we should serve in the newness of the Spirit. Rom. 7:6

* * *

The skepticism of humanity is repressed subconscious. We do not believe there is more than what our conscious mind perceives. The lack of knowledge of the awareness of our subconscious keeps us in bondage which is secular humanism. We need to enter the ground of objectivity and perceive the world like Jesus did with maturity, humility and love; this will awaken the reflective consciousness. Our harried and rushed world often controls our lives, dulling our senses to the supernatural, leaving us insecure and ignorant to the presence of the Almighty. Most people are skeptical of revelation. In our time they find it impossible to believe that God can talk to us like in biblical times.

Even some clergymen will not recognize such phenomenal happenings. There is an article by Pastor Steve Sjogren from Cincinnati, Ohio, in Guideposts, THE VOICE , September 2006, p.76,

Pastor Steve says, **"It might sound strange coming from a pastor, but I always thought that people who said they heard God talking out loud to them were a little kooky."** When Steve had his gall bladder removed, it almost cost him his life. The story stated that something went very wrong with the laparoscopic surgery. The scalpel tore his aorta in two places. He found himself floating above the operating table. He affirms that he was conscious, **"I was, I assure you, totally lucid, with clarity of thought and perception."** He states, that he saw a light that gave him a sense of peace. Steve heard a voice that was strong and clear and definitive as his thoughts. **"Don't worry, Steve. It's going to be okay."** He survived the operation, which was a total miracle. Now he states, **"And I'm not so skeptical when people tell me that they hear God and speak to him,"** The way he explains the whole episode and the conversation he had with God is truly fascinating, inspirational and interesting. Because he is a pastor, the whole story takes on a different quality and credibility. He related his experience to the stories of the Bible, such as what Moses must have felt hearing God's voice on Mount Horeb. Steven Sjogren wrote a book about his enlightening death experience called, <u>The Day I Died.</u>

* * *

Two things fill the mind with ever new and increasing admiration and awe the starry heavens above me and the moral law within me.

Immanuel Kant

Advocate: In the Old Testament the Holy Spirit generally only appeared to selective prophets. After the birth and death of Jesus Christ, the Holy Spirit graciously comes to believers as an advocate to be with us forever. Respectfulness is a must, because the Holy Spirit is not under human control or influences. He is incomparably serious and respectful of our free will, for it is God approaching us with His love.

Jesus instructed the people not to abuse the presence and the manifestation of the **Holy Spirit**.

"Therefore I say to you, every sin and blasphemy will be forgiven men, but the blasphemy against the Spirit will not be forgiven men." Matthew 12:31

People become angry, resentful and even curse against God and Jesus, but the sin against the Holy Spirit is the only unforgivable sin in the Bible. That puts emphasis on the statement the Spirit made to Anton. If we displease, offend and anger the Holy Spirit, He will depart and we will lose the connection with God and Jesus, making us lost forever. As long as we have the connection with the Holy Spirit we are not alienated from God. There will always exist the possibility and the opportunity for reconciliation with God for the rebellious and sinful nature of us human beings. Through repentance and asking for forgiveness we will have the opportunity to gain His mercy. Being alienated from the Holy Spirit is tragic beyond measure, a deadly serious matter. Under no circumstances should we lose contact with the Holy Spirit for its presence is vital for our salvation.

"Do not cast me away from your presence and do not take your Holy Spirit away from me." Ps. 51:11

This information has cemented the fact that one cannot have a relationship with either God or Jesus, without including the Holy Spirit. He is the connection to the other two parts of the Trinity. If we offend the Holt Spirit, we will not be forgiven, no matter how remorseful we are, we are not going to be heard. We have cut the connection to God. There is no magical reconnect button to push when we have offended the Holy Spirit in any manner.

* * *

Respectful: Anton grew bolder during her visits with the Holy Spirit. She was full of spiritual questions, but still tried to be careful, at the same time, in how she expressed herself. She was always polite and respectful. One night, she asked, **"Holy Spirit, exactly where do you come from? We know when Jesus was born, because the Bible substantiates the fact, but what about you?"** The Holy Spirit's vibrations entered her subconscious, and this is what He said, **"I am a Spirit that was created into existence out of the love of God."**

KNOWING GOD THROUGH HIS LOVE WHICH

IS THE ESSENCE OF HIS HOLY, UNCHANGEABLE

NATURE. LOVE IS NOT MERELY AN ATTRIBUTE OF

GOD, BUT HIS NATURE.

That was an overwhelming statement. What better way is there then through His love to communicate with His creation? It is an exciting realization to acknowledge what a fantastic gift God has given to the world, the Holy Spirit, God's love! God must have created the Holy Spirit before He created the universe.

"You send forth Your Spirit, they are created;
And You renew the face of the earth." Psalm 104:30

CREATING LIFE IS THE WORK OF THE

HOLY SPIRIT, THE AGENT IN CREATION

WITH THE FULLNESS OF GOD.

"By the word of the Lord the heavens were made," Psalm 33:6

God as Holy Spirit speaks to us in the deep places of our own spirits and we can respond to Him by our thoughts and lives. We also can speak to Him in prayer and feel assured that He hears, and gives to us companionship, guidance, strength.

Furthermore; the Holy Spirit gives us guidance, with light upon the decisions we must make. The Holy Spirit will not automatically settle our problems for us, for God expects us to use our minds and the best judgment possible about the situation.

Georgia Harkness

The Holy Spirit has all the knowledge and all the power in God's universe and is present everywhere in the universe. The ministry of the Holy Spirit is being the helper of the Almighty. When Jesus was present with the disciples, He told them that in His absence He would pray to the Father, and He will give you another Helper.

"But the helper, the Holy Spirit, whom the Father will
send in My name, He will teach you all things, and bring to
your remembrance all things I said to you." John 14:26

The angel Gabriel told Mary that she would conceive and bring forth a Son, and she should called Him Jesus. Mary could not understand and said to the angel,

"How can this be, since I do not know man?"
And the angel answered and said to her, "The Holy Spirit
will come upon you, and the power of the highest will overshadow
you; therefore, also, that Holy One who is to be born
will be called the Son of God." Luke 1:34-35

The Holy Spirit's accessibility is confirmed by these two Bible scriptures. This proves and establishes that He truly is God's connection to His people here on earth. The Holy Spirit is God's love, made into a spirit, which is part of God's Spirit. An example of this principle would be that God extends Himself to us in love in order to save our souls. The Holy Spirit is God, even though He is a different Spirit. Jesus is also a different Spirit, but was made through the Holy Spirit, which makes Jesus the same actual tangible essence and the same appropriate value as that of God. When the Holy Spirit is in control, all things are possible. The connection makes all three Spirits into one; God Almighty!

The translation of **"Spirit"** in Hebrew and Greek are wind and breath, which are used in the Bible to describe unseen reality. Therefore, wind and breath are symbols of the Holy Spirit just like the dove.

"And John bore witness, saying, I saw the Spirit
descending from heaven like a dove, and it remained upon Him."
John 1:32

Other symbols are oil, fire and living waters. God called the Spirit His Spirit.

"And the Spirit of the God moved upon the face of the waters." Gen. 1:2

The Holy Spirit is God Himself, actually present in Him.

"But they rebelled and grieved His Holy Spirit:
therefore He was turned to be their enemy," Isaiah 63:10

"Teach me to do thy will, for thou art my God: the
Spirit is good: lead me to the land of uprightness." Psalm 143:10

* * *

Relationship: With this continuous running dialogue that Anton had with the Holy Spirit, came numerous ideological questions important and complex issues to find reference to the whole truth. There was one answer that she remembers well, because He told it with such kindness and patience, as if He wanted to make sure that she understood the whole concept. This was the question, **"Holy Spirit, there's an intriguing mystery about the difference between our spirit and our soul. Can you please explain?"** This is how she interpreted the vibrations of the Holy Spirit, **"The soul is the essence of everything you are, and it will continue to exist after death. Your spirit assists you with life and records everything from birth to death of what you do and say including your experiences, all dialogue between you and others, and your perception of life. Your spirit also assists you with your relationship with God."** Then

He added, **"When a human being dies, before the spirit leaves the body, the spirit and soul join together."** He also explained, **"When people report to have near-death- life experiences, and they claim to see their life flashing instantaneously in front of them, what is occurring is the spirit is conjoining with the soul."** Anton was shocked and overwhelmed by the explanation and example, because she was not expecting an explanation so specific in this concept of the inquiry of the soul and spirit, for Him to take the time to make absolutely sure that she understood was beyond her comprehension for quite some time.

For this is God, Our God forever and ever
He will be our guide even to death. Ps. 48:14

* * *

God has everything in control. There is no misunderstanding when we arrive to our destination. It seems we are like a computer, taking all the raw data of our lives with us. Of course, that is just a metaphor, because there is nothing like us on earth. We were manufactured in such an intricate way and the only blueprint in existence like us. The way the human body works is a masterpiece. Some of us have the notion that we can control our own life without considering that we are like a drop of water in the ocean, and God is the ocean. We are made in His image, but in a very small way. That is why He is the Almighty. There is no way for human beings to even contemplate the magnitude **of God**.

Then God said, "Let us make man in Our image, according
to Our Likeness; let them have dominion over the fish of the sea, over
the birds of the air, and over the cattle, over all the earth and
over every creeping thing that creeps on earth." Gen. 1:26

The information that we take with us will determine and help us understand the rewards we will receive in our celestial body. It is truly phenomenal, the process of how God prepares us for our destination after we are deceased. Hopefully, our destination will be to the path of salvation. Perhaps, this will give us a new perspective and a new point of view on how we are supposed to live and direct our lives and the meaning of salvation. Jesus assured His disciples,

And everyone who competes for the prize is temperate in all things. Now they do it to obtain a perishable crown, but we for an imperishable crown. 1 Cor. 9:25

"For My name's sake, shall receive a Hundred fold, and inherit eternal life." Matt. 19:29

Having a deep relationship and His manifestation of His existence in the physical is wonderful and beyond imagination. We are deeply moved. There is no gush of feeling which distracts the thoughts, but the mind sees the truth unveiled. This relation is in such a great degree of understanding that it takes away bodily will. The mind looks in upon the unveiled glories of the Godhead. The veil seems to be removed from the mind and sees the truth very much as we must suppose it to be when the spirit is disembodied. It is no wonder this overpowers our will, over the will of God. The information does not appear to be stultified and confused, but full of light. We find great changes in us that take place. All our interior and outward facilities are conscious of the new strength of mind. Clear perceptions of matters that had before been strange to us are clearer now. Seeing the evident manifestation of the divine truth, a supernatural phenomenon process begins to develop and occur in our lives that we are aware of. For example, we become mentally sharper and discerning of what is good or bad for us. More importantly, prayer, scripture reading, caring for others and love for God begin to increase.

Biblical writings often seem to contradict themselves, but now the light of the Holy Spirit gives us the grace of understanding all scripture. Even passages which have the same meaning are never self-contradictory. Such an example is the parable of the two sons; it is difficult to understand without the assistance of the Holy Spirit.

"A man had two sons, and he came to the first and said," 'Son, go, work today in my vineyard.' "He answered and said," 'I will not, but after regretted it and went.' "Then he came to the second and said likewise. And he answered and said," 'I go, sir,' but he did not go. Matt. 21:28-30

Jesus wants to know which son did the will of the father. Of course we would think the first one did, but that is the wrong answer. God does not want us to serve Him grudgingly and reluctantly, so actually neither son pleased the father.

Having this grace of communion with the Holy Spirit brings responsibility. We must be sure that we are receiving the message and information correctly. We should be respectful, not asking silly questions and treating the Holy Spirit with ultimate respect, because that is exactly how He behaves with us. We must never treat Him like a **"Genie"** (as if He possesses magical powers.) Our requests should be honorable. After all, He is the Father and wants the best for us, just like any normal Father would. God does not let us know any insights we are not ready to hear or handle. Some of us believe and think we can obtain any information we might desire after we have this communication without the consideration that God lives in the present, not in the past or the future. We must not ask for outcomes of events, which can certainly be changed with prayer or our free will. We do have the privilege to ask for guidance on decisions, recognizing that life can bring consequences when judgment about those decisions is incorrect. This is the reason why we should be appreciative for any help the heavenly Father is willing to give us.

When we acquire the precious gift of communication with the Lord, we have the responsibility to use it wisely. We must be grateful and thankful and let the Lord know we will be careful with His bounty. Sometimes if the communication is not clear, we need to remember that when we become more deeply involved in the word of God, the better the connection and enlightenment we have.

It is hard to find words in the language of men to explain 'the deep things of God'. Indeed there are none that will adequately express what the children of God experience.

John Wesley

* * *

Doubts: Human beings seem to complicate beliefs about spiritual theology and are so incredulous that we lose the place in the realm of our thoughts where we can find the central truth of God. We cease giving the attention to our origins, in being made in the likeness of God's image and ignoring the acknowledgment of our rational qualities. We seem, by nature to limit ourselves through are insecurities. We are inclined to restrict and put boundaries in our evolvement not letting our full potential develop. We tend to forget how wonderful God's glory is. We do not use all the skills God has given us; for example, our thoughts and imagination are the architects of things to happen. If we want to achieve a relationship with the Creator we must read and meditate on the word and imagine ourselves communicating with the Lord for it to come to pass.

THERE IS A CONNECTION BETWEEN

KNOWING AND OBEYING GOD. WE HAVE TO BE

WILLING TO LET JESUS INTO OUR LIVES IN ORDER

FOR GOD TO USE US FOR HIS GLORY.

* * *

The word of God is greater than heaven and earth, yes, greater than death and hell, for it forms part of the power of God, and endures everlastingly; we should therefore, diligently study God's word, and know and assuredly believe that God Himself speaks to us.

Martin Luther

Chapter 3

SUFFERING

Christians know not to believe in God out of convenience, because we are Jesus' followers and believers in loving and being devoted to the Father.

"Neither this man nor his parents sinned, but that the works of God should revealed in him." John 9:3

As so often happens with lukewarm Christians as Anton was before she was overcome by the Spirit, when this phenomenal experience occurs we automatically think that we are entitled to special privileges. We do not realize there is a process of involvement. We are incredibly naïve about God's laws. We are unaware that we must be patient as the process of the information enters our subconscious to develop maturity in our spiritual walk.

At the beginning of Anton's revelation of the Holy Spirit, she was watching a program concerning a charismatic nun. The nun was suffering from asthma, and sometimes the condition impaired her speech. She coughed and apologized all the time. Anton, naïve as she was, thought that now with her new encounter she could help the nun. She asked the Holy Spirit, **"If I pray very intensely with all my heart, will the nun be healed?"** It was a good gesture on her part, but the Holy Spirit's vibrations answered, **"No, she is doing penance."** Anton was astonished about this statement and she asked, **"Oh my**

God, what sins has she committed? She looks like such a nice person." There was no answer from the Holy Spirit. He wanted her to ponder on the question. She immediately began mulling this over in her mind and thought there must be another meaning for penance, other than the common meaning of punishment and suffering for committing sins.

Again Anton was watching this early-morning program when the Holy Spirit's vibrations mentioned to her, **"The nun is doing penance for other living souls."** Once more it caught her by surprise and she exclaimed, **"Oh my God, that is terrible!"** She thought, to herself, **"I do not even want to pay for my own sins, much less for somebody else's sins. This is precisely the reason I pray for forgiveness all the time with the Lord's Prayer."**

Why should a person have to suffer for somebody else, especially if we are not even aware that we are martyrs? But, we all know that God does not let anything happen to us that we cannot bear and causes everything to work together for the ultimate good, for His mystical body. God knows His people in advance and which ones are to become like His Son and share His **"Passion."** Paul understood this concept well and knew that whatever happens to us is for our own evolvement. He suggested that through Scripture we can attain patience, comfort and hope. Rom. 15:4

For whom He foreknew, He also predestined to conform
to the image of His Son, He also justified; He also glorified.
Rom. 8:29-30

Bearing Others' Burdens

We then who are strong ought to bear with the scruples
of the weak, and not to please ourselves. Let each of us please his
neighbor for his good, leading to edification. Rom. 15:1-2

* * *

This reminds Anton of her dear friend Pam, who has experienced all kinds of illnesses in the past ten years. Most of the time, she is suffering from one kind of ailment or another. It seems like she is destined to never be in good health again. She is a wonderful human being, a good Christian, fun to be with, charitable, and is not attracted to luxuries, but in spite of these qualities she feels like the black sheep of the family. She feels she causes her bad health in some indirect way. Whether she does or not, she is exactly the way God intended her to be for a purpose.

"Before I formed you in the womb I knew you; Before you were born I sanctified you; I ordained you a prophet to the nations." Jer. 1:5

"Thus says the Lord who made you and formed you from the womb, who will help you." Is. 44:2

You are who you are for a reason. You're part of an intricate plan. You're a precious and perfect unique design, called God's special woman or man. You look like you look for a reason. Our God made no mistake. He knit you together within the womb, You're just what he wanted to make.

Russell Kelfer

* * *

Even though Jesus died for our sins, we still have to repent for our sins and have faith we will be forgiven. Jesus preached the need for repentance. He also required His apostles and disciples to preach on the importance of repenting, which involves the changing of the direction of life not only for ourselves, but for our children and their children, because there are the children that suffer for the sins of their fathers. There is no reason for our sins to escalate to other generations when we have the Holy Spirit within us, and He is with the Father and the Son. Imagine how many future tragedies we will avoid if we **repent often.**

'The Lord is long suffering and abundant in mercy, forgiving iniquity and transgressions; but He by no means clears the guilty, visiting the iniquity of the fathers on the children to the third and fourth generation.' Num. 14:18

My little children, these things I write to you, so you may not sin. And, if anybody sins, we have an Advocate with the Father, Jesus Christ the righteous. 1 John 2:1

* * *

One of the greatest mistakes that we commit is the penchant for judging and condemning people because we do not understand them. Some times we are guilty of not showing compassion for those individuals who by nature have trouble with life, and they do not seem to be able to help themselves. Instead of being helpful we judge them, especially those who are supposedly the black sheep of the family. These individuals may be suffering for the generational sins of the family, current family members or friends. Perhaps they are like the nun, doing penance for mankind in general. It is critical, as Christians, not to judge these individuals until the Lord tells us personally the reason why bad things happen to good people. We really do not know why these Sheep of the Lord are having such a difficult time. This may be completely ordered by God to fulfill His will- not just some difficulty this or that person has gotten into. We must make sure we do not judge; we should pray for these people without ceasing.

WE ARE HERE TO BE JUDGED NOT TO JUDGE.

* * *

We often wonder why little children suffer from cancer or other terrible illnesses. Where is God in all of this, and why does He allow it? Now, at least it makes some sense. These little ones and other souls are not aware that they volunteered and made a commitment before they were conceived and born to follow in Jesus' steps. Suffering takes sins away. The children volunteer to be like Jesus for the good of the world and help us to stay clean (righteous), because we all fall short of His grace. There is an abundance of good will on the other side, so difficult for us to comprehend or conceive. It seems incomprehensible theology, but it is in the Bible even before Jesus Christ.

Yet it pleased the Lord to bruise Him; He has put Him
to grief. By His knowledge My righteous Servant shall justify.
Is. 53:10

This is specifically the reason why God's only Begotten Son came to the world for humanity's sins and to teach us to love each other. It clearly states Christ's crucifixion was a part of God's plan for salvation. Jesus said on the cross, **"It is finished."** That meant His mission and His legacy. His legacy is for us to strive to be like Him and to help each other. This concept was even more understood where He came from than in this world. It was mentioned before that some souls agree to come into this world knowing that they are going to suffer for the benefit of others, without any recollection after conception. This is easily understood when there's really no explanation why some people and children suffer more than others. Religious people who volunteer to give up their lives to Jesus Christ are aware that their suffering is not just some cosmic accident.

Pain takes sins away. It is no wonder then why Jesus suffered such a horrific death. When Jesus cried out to His Father, **"Why hast thou forsaken me?"** It was not that God had forsaken His Son, but rather that Jesus' pain was so intense that He could not endure much more than the Roman soldiers were inflicting upon Him. While on earth He possessed a human body with human feelings. His body felt every torture that was dealt to Him on that day which made Him suffer as much as any other human being might suffer physically.

"And he who does not take his cross and
follow after Me is not worthy of Me." Matt. 10:38

Spirituality is a community enterprise. It is

the passage of people through the solitude and dangers of the desert, as it carves out its own way in the following of Jesus Christ. This spiritual experience is the well from which we must drink.

Gustavo Gutierrez

* * *

Our soldiers are volunteers, and they can end up being martyrs, too. They will suffer for other Americans, preserve our liberty and protect the United States. They do not know if they are going to be in a war and be shot or even killed! The final point to this is these young men and women take an oath to protect the U.S. Their mission is to preserve democracy and our way of life for all Americans. There is something for us to learn from them and their families about our mission here on earth.

The body of Christ: God constantly and persistently tries to help and save His mystical body which is His children and His church. He will gladly accept the sacrifice of any of His children to save his lost Sheep. We Christians are in this mystical body together, whether we are aware of it or like it. There is a story that explains eloquently and precisely the circumstances of how we find ourselves in this mystical body in the world. This story took place in the capital of Siena Province, Tuscany Region, in north central Italy. It was written by Wendy M. White in Part 5, **"Exploring Spiritual Guidance: The Spirit of Christ"** which appears in the book entitled Companions in Christ.

In the fourteenth-century Italy, a remarkable woman named Catherine, who lived in the town of Siena, authored a book entitled The Dialogue. It recorded an account of a conversation between God and "a soul." In it Catherine writes that God speaks of the church as a vineyard in which each individual has his or her own vine garden but in which there are no fences or dividing lines between the gardens. Whatever happens in one's own vineyard, for good or for ill, intimately affects every other vineyard.

Clearly, Catherine of Siena was developing the biblical image of the vine and the branches of which Jesus speaks in John 15. But she did not understand the image in an individualistic way. Not only are we nurtured by a common source-Christ, the Vine-but we are interconnected and thus help nurture one another as well. The fruitfulness of the entire vineyard- the church-is shared by all of us, not only as recipients but as assistant gardeners. Our weeding, pruning, fertilizing, and planting are not only for ourselves; they are for all of us together. Scripture underscores this idea with another metaphor like the church as one body with many members but one Spirit (1Cor.12; Eph.4). Our growth in God is a communal venture!

* * *

In this world it is unavoidable to not suffer in one way or another. This is not being pessimistic; it is a reality because we are together in His mystical body. People have the misconception that God does evil things to mankind to punish us for our evil ways, but nothing could be farther from the truth. God is in total control and His very being will not allow Him to do evil. There will be times when He can step aside to allow man to be taught a lesson to avoid a worse catastrophe for mankind. We are all sinners, and we were all born with original sin and the tendency to sin. He has a tremendous love for us that implies freedom and cannot force us to love Him. He wants created beings to share His life. He does not want us to be like mechanical robots and obey His commands. Our responsibility and remedy is to keep ourselves clean from sin by repenting from our transgressions to transform God's mystical body into a great weapon against the enemy.

HAVING A PURE HEART;

MEANS CLEAN OF STAIN OF SIN.

"Blessed are the pure in heart: for they shall see God." Matt. 5:8

* * *

The blood of Christ: Jesus knew that through His personal suffering and the blood sacrifice of His body, He would be cleansing His followers so that they would be able to enter heaven. We can share this purification of souls through suffering, but ultimately only through Him can our sins be forgiven. Here we are in the 21st Century and still do not realize that He uses suffering to purify the soul. He is making our mind and heart to be pure like a child. Jesus told His disciples when the little children wanted to come to Him,

"Let the little children come to Me, and do not forbid them: for of such is the kingdom of heaven." Matt. 19:14

* * *

We must not let our past sins stop us from getting right with God! The immutable law is that once God has forgiven us of our sins, then He wipes the slate clean and He remembers the sin no more! The shedding of the blood of the lamb-Jesus has taken our black heart and turned it white as snow in God's eyes for everlasting life! None of us knows the exact time or day we will die, but if we have repented of our sins to God, than we will have no fear of death and will be ready to meet God and Jesus any day.

For, "Whoever calls on the name of the Lord shall be saved." Rom. 10:13

* * *

The important point of emphasizing the blood of Jesus in the New Testament is to lead us to the Old Testament that had blood sacrifices on the Day of Atonement. This was a day when Jews used to sacrifice animals to atone for the sins from the previous year for the Jewish Nation as a whole, for the 12 tribes of Israel, each family and individual Jew. They had dreams of some mystical person who would come and lead them to triumphant glory. In an indirect way it came true, because that prophecy was Jesus. God brought Jesus into the world to eventually be a sacrifice for all who believed in Him. He died for all of our sins. The prophecy of the Old Testament came true, and is the reason why the United States helps support the nation of Israel. Christians are in agreement, because our religion was born out of the Jewish religion. Jesus was born a Jew and helped us to become children of the **true God.**

If we say that we have not sin, we deceive ourselves, and the truth is not in us. 1 John 1:8

But if we walk in the light as He is in the light, we have fellowship with one another, and the blood of Jesus Christ His Son cleanses us from all sin. 1 John 1:7

* * *

Anton and Pam went to see Mel Gibson's movie, "The Passion" which was almost too horrible to bear, especially watching how Jesus was tortured by the Romans. The pain He endured could be felt by the entire viewing audience and their moans were as unpalatable as the noises coming from the movie itself.

Anton was apprehensive about going to the movie, because she dislikes showing emotion in public, which she experiences when pain is involved. She asked the Holy Spirit to help her to not become too emotional and not to break down in tears in the theater during the showing of the film. He answered her prayer in an incredible way by saying, **"Anton, do not cross your legs, because it will cut God's protection and then we cannot help you."** It was really miraculous, His grace and protection was flowing through her body, and she did not shed one tear. But by the time she shared this information with Pam, it was too late because Pam had already started to cry and could not stop. It is amazing that small things like not crossing our legs will help some people in their protection and communication with the Lord. We need to remain open-minded and receptive to His presence.

O you mighty ones, Give unto the Lord the Glory due to His name; Worship the Lord in the beauty of His holiness. The voice of the Lord is over the waters; The voice of the Lord is powerful; the voice of the Lord is full of majesty. The voice of the Lord breaks the cedars, The voice of the Lord makes the deer give birth. And in His temple everyone says, "Glory!" The Lord will give strength to His people; The Lord will bless His people with peace. Ps. 29:1-5, 9, 11

It is normal for Christians to experience ups and downs in our lives with different durations and intensities. It seems like life is full of beginnings and endings, times of joy and times of sadness. They are normal spiritual experiences. God allows such alterations in our lives, because some souls profit by tribulations for purification. There is always a reason for the Father allowing transgressions to take place. It is either to guide us to a different direction or there is something to learn from the occurrence about the vision God has for us.

Paula White says about transgressions, "If it is not God sent it is God used." In other words if the enemy transgresses against us, God uses it for good.

* * *

When the morning's freshness has been replaced by the weariness of midday, when the leg muscles quiver under the strain, the climb seems endless, and suddenly, nothing will go quite as you wish it is then that you must not hesitate.

Dag Hammarskjold

"It is not for you to know times or seasons which the Father has put in His own authority. But you shall receive power when the Holy Spirit has come upon you: and you shall be witnesses to Me." Acts 1:7-8

Vibrations

The Holy Spirit has begun a more extensive work with humanity. The essence of His doctrine carries the authority of God just as it has for centuries.

"All flesh is grass, And all the glory of man as the flower of the grass. The grass withers, And its flower falls away, But the word of the Lord endures forever." 1 Pet. 1:24-25

When people are bilingual, similar to Anton, they switch languages back and forth, especially if they know the other person they are talking to speaks the same languages. They also do it in their thinking. Talking to the Lord is very much like thinking. We communicate through thoughts. Anton noticed that every time she spoke to the Holy Spirit in Spanish or English, the Holy Spirit responded to her in the language that she had used to address Him. She asked Him, **"Why do You answer me in the same language that I used when I asked You the question?"** The questions were usually about finding the reference to the whole truth about some complex issues of God's laws.

The Holy Spirit answered, **"Anton, it is your brain that is translating the words in the language of the question"** God addresses us by our first name or our nickname, the same as He did to the people in the times of the Bible. He went further by saying, **"We (the Holy Trinity) communicate with people through vibrations."** Now, He must consider this to be an important message, because His answers are usually with one sentence unless the question is significant. We cannot engage in a conversation with the Holy Spirit. To disclose such a matter, would be deceiving and insincere. If it was not for the manifestation of the touching that Anton receives, she would not believe that she is actually hearing these messages or communicating with the Spirit. What she does is she repeats what is being conveyed, and asks the Holy Spirit to move her head to a **"yes"** or a **"no"**, to confirm if the comprehension and translation is absolutely correct. Another interesting fact is knowing the solutions and results to situations and matters that were difficult to us before. Now the answers are transcended into our mind with the knowledge and wisdom of the Holy Spirit. By this time, our consciousness has developed an understanding of how to comprehend and interpret the answers, considering and accepting that they (the Holy Trinity) operate in a different orbit, and their laws are not our Laws where there is no time or space. The Holy Spirit is working on the border between the Spiritual realm and physical realm.

O LORD, You have searched me and know me. If I ascend into heaven, You are there; If I make my bed in hell, behold, You are there.
Ps. 139:1, 8

* * *

When we acquire a relationship with God and understand the vibrations of the Holy Spirit, we become one, our spirit with His Spirit. He knows what we are thinking, what we are going to say and what we are going to ask. But, it is difficult to realize that we have achieved this Spiritual transition and conversion, because interpreting the vibrations can be extremely complicated, such as translating the vibrations to our own language, and our own comprehension. It is sort of a set back, because we think we are talking to ourselves, when actually God is talking to us. When Jesus prayed for the Disciples He asked the Holy Father,

"Through Your name those whom You have given Me, that they may be one as we are one." John 17:11

Peter's sermon, to the people of Judea was about what the prophet Joel had spoken of about what God had said,

"That I will pour out My Spirit on all flesh; your sons and your daughters shall prophesy, your young men shall see visions, your old men shall dream dreams." Acts 2:17

The real content of revelation in the Bible is not "something," but God Himself. Revelation is self-manifestation of God. The real revelation with which the whole Bible is concerned, is God's self-manifestation.

Emil Brunner

* * *

Finding and understanding God's plan automatically makes life not so complicated and confusing. Say, for example, a woman desires to conceive and have a baby, and she is having trouble getting pregnant. This is a very difficult position to be in. And suppose she has a relationship with the Lord. Then she could ask the Lord, **"What can I do? Should I consider fertilization?"** The Lord will advise her about what she should do if she is destined to conceive and have a child. If her fate is not to have a child by natural means, then she knows not to waste her time and money plus the pain she would have to endure. Perhaps, she is predestined to adopt a child. There are so many little ones that need a home and somebody to love them. This is where the free will comes in; she can decide to adopt or not to adopt. Some women feel that it is unfair. Why can they not have a child of their own and conceive? God's love is unfathomable. We must trust His judgment and will to dispose and dispense everything for our own goodwill. We must accept His freedom and will.

THERE IS NOTHING EARNED,

EVERYTHING IS A GIFT AND GRACE FROM THE LORD.

"Is it not lawful for me to do what I wish with my own things?" Matt. 20:15

* * *

When we are able to understand the vibrations of the Holy Spirit, we feel it is absolutely imperative and necessary to accept the will of God. For the gratitude for this honor of being close to the Lord, we feel privileged and would not dare question His will. Some people have the misconception that we can change God's will, especially, when we have this communication, not realizing that this is when we should feel that it is even more imperative and vital to be obedient to His will.

Grace is never merely the setting aside of condemnation but the royal bestowal of gifs at the banquet; the granting of the Highest good, eternal life (Rom.5:21). Of course, grace, like faith, leads only to the threshold of this last thing of all, the divine glory (2 Cor. 5:7; 12:9).

Emil Brunner

It can become extremely confusing at times, when we are trying to make a distinction between the vibrations coming into our subconscious. The idea here is to concentrate, analyze and examine our thoughts, asking for assistance from God to help us differentiate our own thoughts from the Holy Spirit vibrations and the enemy's vibrations. Being able to recognize the Holy Spirit vibrations will be enormously and exceedingly beneficial to our everyday life, because He will never lead us along the wrong path. This acknowledgement will lead us to capture God's concern for our affairs and to appreciate the essence of God in action, understanding His integrity and the love He has for us. God has a specific purpose for our journey in this world without affecting human freedom. He is ultimately respectful of free will. We are predestined to live out the plan He has for us; it is up to us to accept His plan. Most believers experience tremendous satisfaction and fulfillment by accomplishing His divine purpose.

"But you are a chosen generation, a royal priesthood, a holy nation, His own special people, that you may proclaim the praises of Him who called you out of darkness into His marvelous light."
1Peter 2:9

To actually learn to recognize the word of the Lord and to have a relationship with the creator is seriously a wondrous grace. This state of grace should be embraced with passion and trust without thinking that such disclosure is self-delusional. We should not let unhealthy vibrations make us feel that God Is hidden and inaccessible and it is illogical for us to possibly hope to know God and have a relationship with Him. The belief here is to be objective and have the certainty that God is ultimately and clearly beyond our ken.

"The word is near you, in your mouth and in your heart."
Rom. 10:8

Your ears shall hear a word behind you, saying, "This is the way, walk in it." Is. 30:21

We sense the reality of God within us, a light from inside ourselves. Intersecting in a complex way, our spirit is intricately interwoven with the Holy Spirit. He will approach us through any avenue we are willing to open and being perceptive to His divine presence. This experience will transcend us to independence from this world without being apologetic for this phenomenal understanding.

These divine vibrations coming from the Holy Spirit are intellectually challenging, which calls us to reason with our senses, making the presupposition of believing in the reality of God. It is like walking into the sunlight and opening our eyes and declaring personally that the God of Jesus Christ is our God.

"For this very purpose I have raised you up,
that I may show My power in you, and that My
name may be declared in all the earth." Rom. 9:17

Jesus Christ is himself God as the Son of God the Father and with God the father the source of the Holy Spirit, united in one essence with the Holy Spirit.
That is how He is God. He is God as He takes part in the event which constitutes the divine being.

Karl Bar

Understanding: When a person is receiving the Holy Spirit's vibrations and is trying to decode them, then the clarification, translation and the authenticity of the vibrations greatly depends on the person's ability to decode the vibration's information correctly. For example, a popular Christian minister at one time claimed that if he did not raise one million dollars for his ministry, God told him that he would die. Some people were outraged by that claim, because it is difficult to think God would put anybody in such a dilemma, even though he did raise the million dollars for his ministry; it was still difficult to believe. Perhaps, the minister misunderstood the information. Decoding the vibrations of the Holy Spirit is an extremely sensitive matter, especially if we are to share this information with other people.

We must not underestimate the power of our mind that is made in the likeness of God; it possesses creative and divine intelligence. The depths of our mind can tap into the infinite power within us, enabling us and inspiring us with wisdom and understanding of the psychological truth. The way to tune into these vibrations is by learning to reach a meditative state when we are not awake or asleep. That is when we are more sensitive to this information. It is a way to quiet our minds, penetrating into the depths of our subconscious and discovering the mysteries of our existence.

Do not neglect the gift that is in you, Meditate on these things;
give yourself entirely to them, that your progress may be evident to all.
Take heed to yourself and to the doctrine. Continue in them, for in
doing this you will save both yourself and those who hear you.
1 Tim. 4:14-16

When we concentrate and meditate on the word of the Lord, we leave our problems that overwhelm us behind giving us the ability to appreciate the contents of our subconscious, but at the same time, having control of our thoughts and mind which gives us knowledge of His wisdom and the understanding of a connection that has taken place. When we are asleep, this connection also takes place, but we are not in control of our conscious mind. The information we are receiving is difficult to articulate, because it is blurred and foggy. Consequently, when we dream we do not understand our dreams or the information that is received.

The definition of the word "vibration" from the Oxford Reference Dictionary --the revised 2nd edition. Edited by Judy Pearsall and Bill Trumble.

Vibration: the act or the instance of vibrating; oscillation 2.Physics-- (esp.) rapid motion to and fro, and (esp.) of the parts of elastic, solid whose equilibrium which has been disturbed or an electro-magnetic wave. 3a. a mental (esp. i, occult) influence a characteristic atmosphere or a feeling in a place, regarded as communicable to people in it.

* * *

These vibrations are similar to mental telepathy. Because it is a silent voice, it is for that precise reason, it is essential to have divine intervention to understand correctly and exactly how the Holy Spirit connects with the human spirit. We need assistance to differentiate between His voice and our own thoughts. Learning to differentiate vibrations will be a powerful weapon against the enemy too. Recognizing the Holy Spirit's voice, our mind automatically will not let any other vibrations go through. We must stay vigilant and aware that the enemies' vibrations can and will convince us to do offensive things to ourselves and others that are not pleasing to the Lord. Accepting the information of the Holy Spirit will strengthen our character with purity and fire, transforming us into better beings by the ecstasy of being close to the Lord.

The definition of the word "revelation", in the Nelson's Compact Bible Dictionary By Ronald F. Youngblood, F. F. Bruce and R.K. Harrison.

God's communication to His people concerning Himself,

His moral standards, and His plan of salvation. God is a personal Spirit distinct from the world; He is absolutely holy and is invisible to the view of physical, finite, sinful minds. Although people, on their own, can never create truth about God, God has graciously unveiled and manifested Himself to mankind. Other religions and philosophies result from the endless human quest for God; Christianity results from God's quest for lost mankind God has made Himself known to all people everywhere in the marvels of nature and in human conscience, which is able to distinguish, right from wrong. Because His knowledge is universal and continuous, by it God has displayed His glory to everyone (Ps. 19:1-6.)

* * *

When we learn to recognize the Holy Spirit's vibrations, it will lead us to God and in search of His divine quest and experiencing the acknowledgement of God's presence. The revelation of God will be finally proven to us. Revelation means "an uncovering" from the Latin word revelatio. When we communicate with the Father, Son and the Holy Spirit, together they will guide us to the whole truth.

THE TRUTH WILL SET YOU FREE.

When we find the truth of the evolution of the family of God, it will give us the ability to see the whole picture of life, making us feel a sense of freedom. After He reveals Himself to us, He lets us know the plan He has for our life. He will not reveal too much about what is ahead of us or reveal the future. Patience is required for this communication, for there is a process for revelation and our mind needs to be renewed. We will find out the deep thoughts of God, and having this information will change our lives forever. There will not be any doubt in our minds of what we are supposed to do. It is an experience beyond belief to have the confirmation of the Holy Spirit that we are honoring God's will.

"That He would show you the secrets of wisdom!" Job 11:6

"With Him are wisdom and strength, He has counsel and understanding."
Job 12:13

* * *

Being able to hear these vibrations is dramatically unexplainable. Anton is not trying to convince anybody of this whole equation. It is up to the Holy Spirit to convince whomever He wants to be a believer. The Holy Spirit is the one in charge. This book is just delivering a message.

When we are able to differentiate His vibrations, it reminds us of the verse,

"Be still, and know that I am God." Ps. 46:10

GOD WILL RENEW OUR MINDS TO THE

GREATNESS THAT HE HAS FOR US TO EXTEND

HIS KINGDOM. HE WANTS TO TALK TO OUR HEARTS,

SO WE CAN EXERCISE AND REPRODUCE HIS WORD.

"Then you will be able to test and approve what
God's will is his good, pleasing and perfect will." Rom. 12:2

It is wonderful to understand how God communicates with humans. His language is universal. No matter what language we speak, our brain will translate His language through vibrations to that language. When we learn to recognize His voice that does not mean that we should not use our mind. He still wants us to be our own person. Our human understanding finds it difficult to grasp and realize that we have a counselor within us whenever we need advice. In the beginning of the relationship with the Holy Spirit Anton found herself forgetting to ask for advice when she made important decisions. When her decisions turned out to be wrong, then she realized all she had to do was ask. This concept tells us to be objective and to keep an open mind in seeking and pursuing the understanding of the truth, which is God.

"Your word is a lamp to my feet and a light to my path" Ps. *119:105*

* * *

Since our subconscious mind is receiving the vibrations, it is wise to understand how our subconscious mind works. This was stated before in the book written by Dr. Joseph Murphy, The Power of Your Subconscious Mind. He explains that our subconscious mind can work miracles in our lives and can bring mental healing in these modern times. He also articulates the importance of sleep that collects infinite counseling from the Lord without any recollection but nevertheless it stays in our subconscious.

* * *

An interesting article about sleep, "A New Research on What Your Dreams Really Mean." by Michael J. Weiss appeared in the Reader's Digest of February 2006.

Psychologists have long known that people can solve their problems at work and at home by 'sleeping on it.' The challenge has always been to train yourself to dream up the solutions. Deirdre Barrett, Ph. D. and assistant Psychologist at Harvard Medical School, and an editor of the journal, "Dreaming," advises individuals to ponder questions just before falling asleep. "Should I take this job?" "Should I marry that guy?" And let the subconscious provide the answers.

Some researchers believe that you can guide your dreams while you are sleeping. In recent years Stephen La Berge, Ph.D., has pioneered the way of directing the sleeping mind through "lucid dreams", in which a sleeping person realizes he\she is dreaming, while it is happening.

According to La Berg, lucid dreamers can use the experience for a variety of purposes, problem solving, developing creative ideas and healing. Patricia Keelin, a 55 year old, graphic cartographer, from Norton California, has lucid dreaming for everything from talking to her long-dead father, to diving to the bottom of the ocean without worrying about breathing or (her swimming skills.) "It's exhilarating," she says. "Lucid dreaming is great because it's free and available to everybody."

La Berg says, well, not entirely free. Although everyone has the potential to dream lucidity, it rarely happens routinely without special training or temperament. The Lucidity Institute operates instructional workshops and retreats to spread the gospel.

* * *

And one can never forget the dream that gave Jesus Christ His earthly father Joseph. When this wise man found out that Mary was with the child of the Holy Spirit he was not willing to make her a public example; therefore, he was faced with a difficult dilemma of what to do with her. The story is that in the times of Mary and Joseph it was customary to arrange marriages. According to their law, at fourteen years old Mary was of marriageable age. This decision was initiated by guardians of the Temple Virgins. These virgins had made a vow of virginity.

The priest of the temple announced that Joseph was to be the groom of Mary. Joseph had also reached the age of marriage which was thirty years of age for men. They were to receive a bride to be their faithful companion. Mary was brought forth to meet Joseph and agreed on this decisive proposal. Mary was consigned to Joseph by the priest's orders and arrangement. Their engagement was to live separately in a state of espousal agreement, which usually lasted one year in Galilee. In that year Mary became pregnant by the Holy Spirit. The angel Gabriel was sent by God to notify Mary that she had found **favor with God.**

Then the angel said to her, "Do not be afraid Mary.

Behold, you will conceived in your womb and bring forth a Son, and shall call His name Jesus." Luke 1:30-31

When Joseph found out about Mary's pregnancy he felt it would not be honorable for him to assume paternity of the child; in the view of the requirements of justice of the Mosaic Law. This was a difficult dilemma for this upright man to decide what to do, because even in private a divorce in the presence of a few witnesses would eventually expose Mary to suspicion of adultery. He knew that adultery was usually punished with death by stoning. Perhaps, he could put her away secretly?

But while he thought about these things, behold, the angel of the Lord appeared unto him in a dream, saying, "Joseph, son of David do not be afraid to take unto thee Mary thy wife: for that which is conceived in her is of the Holy Spirit. And she shall bring forth a Son, and thou shall call His name Jesus: for He shall save His people from their sins." Matt. 1:20-21

Joseph was indeed needed for this mission, since he belonged to the line of David. Jesus was introduced into the Davidic line through the divine selection of Joseph as His legal father to fulfill the prophecy of the Old Testament.

Unto us a Child is born, unto us a Son is given; And the government will be upon on His shoulder And His name will be called Wonderful, Counselor, Mighty God, Everlasting Father, Prince of Peace. Is. 9:6-7

* * *

Anton had an MRI and a brain scan, because she suffers from migraine headaches. The tests showed that her brain waves were higher than normal, which is very common in those who suffer from migraine headaches or somebody that suffers from epilepsy, a medical disorder involving episodes of irregular electrical discharge in the brain. They seem to have higher antennas than most people, so to speak, and pick up electricity in the environment. She figures it is probably the reason why her conscious mind can translate the vibrations coming into her subconscious mind while she is awake. She does not even have to get to a meditative state of mind. In spite of the pain that she experiences, she would never trade her ability for anything in this world. It seems that there is a price for everything.

Paul the apostle mentions a thorn in his flesh. Concerning his infirmity, the precise nature of the affliction can only be conjectured; efforts of the identification have varied widely. Paul only said that a messenger of Satan was given to him to buffet him, but never gave the nature of the afflictions. He pleaded with the Lord three times that it might depart from him. In 2 Cor. 12:9 the Lord said to him,

"My grace is sufficient for you, for My strength is made perfect in weakness."

> Paul said *"Therefore most gladly I will rather boast in my infirmities, that the power of Christ may rest upon me. Therefore I take pleasure in my infirmities, in reproaches, in needs, in persecutions, in distresses, for Christ's sake. For when I am weak, then I am strong." 2 Cor. 12:9-10*

* * *

Our goal as Christians should be to seek a direct relationship with the living God, experiencing His knowledge and love, advancing in the mystery until the mystery vanishes leaving us with His essence. This is an existential union with the profound realization of His essence flowing into our heart, giving us the exact definition of a precious relationship taking place. Our senses will be full of admiration, commitment and surrender all intertwined to the deepest corner of our soul. To experience this, is to have concrete evidence of His existence. This dynamic concept will transform us with strength in our faith, recognizing His essential purity.

The Lord My Shepherd

The Lord is my shepherd; I shall not want. He makes me to lie down in green pastures; He leads me beside the still waters. He restores my soul; He leads me in the paths of righteousness for His name's sake. Yea, though I walk through the valley of shadow of death, I will fear no evil; For You are with me; Your rod and Your staff, they comfort me. You prepare a table before me in the presence of my enemies; You anoint my head with oil; My cup runs over. Surely goodness and mercy shall follow me all the days of my life; And I will dwell in the house of the Lord forever. Ps. 23:1-6

The strongest human beliefs arise from the profoundly invisible reality of God. No man can become self-realized without belief in immortal soul The fulfilling of human destiny depends upon what we have become aware of and what our soul has done with it.

Valerie V. Hunt

Your hands have made and fashioned me; Give me understanding, that I may learn Your commandments. Those who fear You will be glad when they see me, Because I have hoped in Your word. I know, O Lord, that Your judgments are right, And that in faithfulness You have afflicted me. Let, I pray, Your merciful kindness be for my comfort, According to Your word to Your servant. Let Your tender mercies come to me, that I may live; For Your law is my delight. Ps. 119:73-77

Supernatural Kingdom

Jesus purchased the kingdom of God with His blood. He purchased the kingdom for the believer, because to Him we are a Pearl of Great Price.

"Again, the kingdom of heaven is like a merchant seeking beautiful pearls. Who, when he had found one pearl of great price, went and sold all that he had and bought it." Matt. 13:45-46

Not everyone is given the same capacity for spiritual growth in the kingdom of God. Any method for advancing should be considered. We must search for any avenue that we can take, for we do not know what unfathomable way will take us to the mystery of God's grace in the world. Just like any human development, it takes dedication, information and much effort. Although we think prayer should cover any situation, there is still much to learn through the Bible and meditating on the word. We should not let the power of the blind forces of the world prevent us from the mystical divinities of God. The kingdom of God is within reach, where there is happiness, peace and joy in the Holy Spirit. Although God sees us like a great pearl, actually the kingdom of God is the greatest treasure. It comes to us through a form of mystery, like a small pearl of great value that can be hidden in one's pocket. Only God can mysteriously reveal this triumphal bliss hidden in us. John the Baptist announced that the kingdom of God was **"at hand"** in the person of Jesus. Jesus claimed that the kingdom of God dawned through His ministry.

"What is the kingdom of God like? And to what shall I compare it ?It is like a mustard seed, which a man took and put it in his garden; and it grew and became a large tree." Luke 13:18

WE NEED TO PURSUE GOD'S

KINGDOM HERE ON EARTH.

The kingdom of God is organic, meaning it grows when fertilized with faith, reading His word and doing His will. Studying God's supernatural interaction with the human race will actively lead us into a higher plane of knowing, being and believing. Our lives will immeasurably become richer through inspirational events. This aspect and concept is not to be feared, for God is extremely careful with us humans. It does not mean experiences with visions or unexplained messages. He knows our limitations, strength and fears. He respects our individual characteristics and our insecurities. When we sincerely seek His guidance and assistance, He will certainly get involved in our lives, delicately preparing the ground for our benefit with circumstances. Sometimes we are not even aware of His involvement. For example, say we commit ourselves to a project and later on we are sorry and resent the fact that we agreed to the commitment. Suddenly, we get a call that the project has been canceled. We say **"thank you God"** without really paying attention. Our busy lives and the noises of the material world do not allow us to recognize God's involvement in our every day lives. It is amazing how God constantly uses His wisdom, guiding our senses and intuitions without interfering with our independence. It is difficult to understand how the supernatural kingdom of God is involved in the life of the believer.

"The kingdom of heaven is like leaven, which a woman took and hid in three measures of meal till it was all leavened." Matt. 13:33

Born thy people to deliver, Born a child a yet a King, Born to reign in us for ever, Now thy gracious kingdom bring. By Thine own eternal Spirit Rule in all our hearts alone; Raise Thine all-sufficient merit Raise us to thy glorious throne.

Charles Wesley

* * *

The message here is to convey how Christians can have a break through into the supernatural, to awaken our senses to spirituality and mysticism. We can ponder on the mysteries of the Bible and find great aid in our Christian awakening by being meticulous in our concentration on God's skillful exposition of the material that His word illustrates. It will help us with discernment of the spirit realm guiding us to a relatively complete understanding. Our spirit will have the certainty of exactly what to discern in our lives and provide us with sound understanding of God's will. Christians with some background in mysticism, contemplation and a deep relationship with the Lord will be able to absorb the material illustrated in this message. Perhaps they will agree that an average person can enjoy the experience of having a break though into the supernatural realm of God, not just reserved for individuals with scholarly credentials.

Again, the kingdom of heaven is like a dragnet that was cast into the shore and gathered some of every kind. Which, when it was full, they drew to shore; and sat down and gathered the good into vessels, and threw the bad away." Matt. 13:47-48

The character in this story arrived into God's supernatural kingdom by meditating on the Lord's Prayer. But everyone's fundamental life of faith is unique. Each journey toward God is completely different, God's relationship and interaction with His family varies. This is precisely the reason for all of this information on different subjects; hopefully, it will assist somebody with spiritual clarity. The frontier is open for the spiritual richness that will strengthen and deepen our faith. By finding the untouched peace of God, our anxieties will be overshadowed by joy, and fear will be replaced with **hope.**

Be anxious for nothing, but in everything by prayer and supplication, with thanksgiving, let your request be made known to God; and the peace of God, which surpasses all understandings, will guard your hearts and minds through Christ Jesus. Phil. 4:6-7

The opportunity is open to infinite possibilities of the human potential. The discovery of the physical and emotional happening in the mysterious subconscious mind is a break through for the soul of a seeker in the awareness of the Spirit that is alive in all of us. It is a fascinating mystical experience for those looking for answers and a deeper understanding of the profound human capacity to function in the spiritual and material realms simultaneously. Our infinite soul and mind can reveal monumental transactions between our mind and God. When we are able to understand the mystery of the vibrations in our mind; new insights will be revealed as well as old insights that are expressed in parables in the Bible.

Jesus said to them, "Have you understood all these things?"
They said to Him "Yes Lord" Then He said to them, "Therefore
every scribe instructed concerning the kingdom of heaven is like a
householder who brings out of his treasure things new and old.
Matt. 13:51-52

* * *

The human conscious mind should be studied to clarify its involvement in our philosophical system. It seems we are not interested in anything if it is not material or substance, as if we are just carnal. We are spiritual beings with speculative systems that could be explored and become extremely profitable to our existence. The realm of pure thought exists and is very real. We are disadvantaged because there have not been many logical studies of metaphysics and this phenomenal nature has not been explored. If we were to examine the subconscious mind of man, we would come out with an adequate explanation of the interaction of humans and God.

Dr. Valerie V. Hunt is the author of Infinite Mind: Science of the Human Vibrations of the Consciousness. She presents the first comprehensive human energy field model based on her 25 years of sophisticated electronic field research and extensive clinical studies. It clarifies metaphysical deductions from physics, evaluates clinical suppositions and should supersede the ancient inadequate explanations of the past.

Dr. Hunt is internationally recognized for her pioneering research of the human energy fields. Her highly creative approach and meticulous research bring together overlapping truths from disciplines. Holding advanced degrees in psychology and physiological science from Columbia University, Dr. Hunt has been a professor at Columbia University of Iowa and in Los Angeles at the University of California. She writes about in the following:

A MIND'S JOURNEY

Have you ever become lost in an enthrallingly beautiful daydream or imagery so frightening that you crashed back to ordinary attention, needing time for things to straighten out so that you could separate yourself from the dream? Perhaps you never did. Such experiences fade rapidly from memory so that you can't even remember what the dream is about. It is easy to pass off these happenings as your imagination having "play time" or to attribute them to fatigue. But deep down is a nagging thought that the dream portrayed a vital part of you that was attempting to surface. Such experiences are common to us humans.

Dr Hunt is to be admired, because she has stood against some beliefs, the organization of science about her clinical work and her strong belief about what she considers to be truth. It takes a strong character to not only believe, but to actually take the time to demonstrate the human energetic system and the educational investigation of human vibrations from a scientific point of view; thus, demonstrating there is a physical and emotional happening in the mysterious energy of the mind. But we do not have to be a professor of science to be able to open ourselves to the infinite possibilities of the human potential. As proven in this book, all we need is faith and God's willingness to help us; for a fascinating mystical experience of the understanding of the profound human capability to function in the spiritual and material realms simultaneously. Dr. Hunt ends her book with stimulating and inspiring words,

Science and spirituality started together and diverged for many centuries. Now they are coming back together. Two of the greatest forces in human thoughts are science and spirituality. Lederman, one of our eminent particle physicists, said, "I think we're on the threshold of finding God--- or at least higher glory. We haven't found it yet, but even science is looking in the right direction." Science has given us new insights that as our field grows in vibrational complexity, as we maintain its dynamic position on the ridge of chaos, our God-like nature will dominate our consciousness and our life.

* * *

"Then the righteous will shine forth as the sun in the kingdom of their Father. He who has ears to hear, let him hear." Matt. 13:43

Chapter 4

COMMITMENT

The purpose for transgressions in this world is to strengthen our character. As our character becomes stronger we learn to trust God and to be committed to Him.

"Foxes have holes and birds of the air have nests, but the Son of Man has nowhere to lay His head." Matt. 8:20

Now it is time for Anton to fulfill her commitment to the Holy Spirit by writing a spiritual book. She has accumulated all this information from her new intimate relationship with Him, but she does not know where to start. Of course, she has her book on how to write a novel and a computer that she bought at the insistence of the Spirit. He assured her she could learn to use it. Most people are not good at reading directions. They have to be shown how things are done, and she is not an exception to the norm. The more she kept rationalizing and analyzing the project, the more difficult and impossible it seemed. She told the Holy Spirit, **"I cannot do this!"**

"O you of little faith. But seek first the kingdom of God
and His righteousness, and all these things shall be added to you."
Matt. 6:30, 33

"And my God shall supply all your need
according to His riches in glory by Jesus Christ." Phil. 4:19

The Holy Spirit's vibration suggested that Anton ask her friend Pam to help her. She thought, **"Oh my God, that is going to be so embarrassing. How am I going to tell this religious woman who has studied the Bible for twenty years and has two master's degrees that God has chosen little old me to write a spiritual book, and oh, by the way, do you mind helping me?"** She told the Spirit, **"I can tell you now, that is not going to go well. She is going to think I'm delusional and nuts."** But, trying to be obedient to His request, she started mulling over in her head different ways on how to approach Pam. She asked the Spirit if she could at least say to her that she was talking to angels. Now with the spiritual new wave and new area, it sounded a little more credible. To her surprise, the Holy Spirit agreed. She interpreted the vibrations as saying, **"Yes"** to her request and He also added, **"When God's angels talk to Humans, I'm the One that makes it possible."**

There is a book called, Angels: God's Secret Agents by Billy Graham. The book stresses how the Bible teaches us the reality and existence of angels, and also the way they intervene and help in the affairs of God's people. Billy Graham says, **"They are spiritual creatures without a physical body, created by God, for the service of Christendom."**

* * *

Pam was interested in what Anton said, because Pam is one of those Christians with blind faith. God has not revealed Himself to them yet.

"Blessed are those who have not seen and yet believed." John 20:29

Jesus was referring to the disbelief of the disciple Thomas, known as **"doubting Thomas,"** because of his inability to believe that Jesus had risen from the dead. He was not present when Jesus first appeared to His disciples after the resurrection. Thomas said,

"Unless I see in His hands the print of the nails, and put my finger

into the print of the nails, and put my hand into the His side, I will not believe." And after eight days His disciples were again inside, and Thomas with them. Jesus came, the doors being shut, and stood in the midst, and said, "Peace to you!" Then He said to Thomas, "Reach your finger here, and look at My hands; and reach your hand here, and put it into My side. Do not be unbelieving, but believing,"
John 20:25-27

Only when he touched Jesus' wounds did he really believe that indeed it was Jesus. Christians who do not actually experience demonstrations of His existence and still believe are sure to be blessed.

* * *

It took time before Pam finally believed Anton was telling the truth about hearing from the spiritual realm. Anton was becoming frustrated and discouraged. She could feel Pam was really not interested in helping her. She was skeptical of Anton's story that angels, through the Holy Spirit, were telling her to write a spiritual book. For Pam it was too unreal for her to take in; however, she did not believe Anton was lying. She would say, **"I believe that you believe what you are saying is true."** Anton loves to laugh, and she laughed at that response, because it was a nice way of saying, **"I do not believe you."**

Anton kept thinking about how she could convince Pam that she was telling the truth. She asked the Holy Spirit, **"What if I put my hands on her and pray to God to let her feel Your presence, like I experienced it?"** The vibrations of the Holy Spirit answered, **"Yes."** It is so difficult to be talking to Somebody you do not see, that even in her own mind she is always questioning that this is actually happening. She was afraid when she would lay hands on Pam that nothing would happen, and she would make a fool of herself. But she had to trust that the Lord would give her power beyond herself.

"You shall receive power when the Holy Spirit has come upon you."
Acts 1:8

THE HOLY SPIRIT WILL WORK IN AN

UNNOTICEABLE GENTLE WAY; HOWEVER, HE CAN

ALSO WORK IN A TUMULTUOUS OUTPOURING WAY,

OVERWHELMING US WITH HIS GRACE.

* * *

Anton took the opportunity one day when Pam came for a hair cut and happened to be the last customer. They always talked about the Lord, so it was easy to ask Pam if she would let her lay her hands and pray to see if she could feel the presence of the Lord. Pam said **"Sure"** When Anton placed her hands on her and prayed, **"Please God, let Pam feel your presence through the Holy Spirit that abides in us and is the advocate of Your Son Jesus who helps us glorify His name."** Anton felt a rush of energy that came through her body transmitting it to Pam. Pam exclaimed, **"Wow, it felt like an electrical current was flowing through my body! What a miraculous and marvelous gift God has given you that you can transmit this power!"** She also said, **"A feeling of tranquility and peacefulness came over me too."** Anton was just as astonished as Pam. This was the first time she ever laid hands on and prayed on somebody.

For you see your calling, brethren, that not many wise according
to the flesh, not many mighty, not many noble, are called. But God has
chosen the foolish things of the world to put to shame the wise, and God has chosen
the weak things of the world to put to shame the things which are mighty.
1 Corinthians 1:26-27

He deigns His influence to infuse,
sweet, refreshing, as the silent dews.

John Wesley

* * *

After that incident, Pam suggested that Anton come to her apartment and they would begin writing the book. Anton was thrilled, Pam had a computer, could type fast, had a master's degree in English and knew the Bible. It should be smooth sailing. Nothing worth doing is easy. To her surprise, when she arrived at the apartment, the first thing the Holy Spirit told her, **"You need to get rid of two things in this apartment."** Thank God Pam did not object. She said, **"By all means, get rid of them."** The Holy Spirit directed Anton to a file cabinet. In the bottom drawer Pam had newspaper clippings of some delinquent bank robbers she had counseled from 1972-1974 when she was working for the Juvenile Probation Department. She intended to write about them once she retired. What was so unique about this case was that these delinquent criminals were so young. One of them was only twelve years old and was the youngest known bank robber in the U.S. at the time. Then, in her bedroom she had fifteen Molas (Panama folk art) hanging on the wall. There was one in particular that the Holy Spirit did not think was pleasing to the Lord. Perhaps, it was the design which was a zigzag pattern of yarn. Pam did not know what these Molas signified; she just knew the art was expensive and beautiful. It is common that we bring things home that are pleasant to the eye without knowing the significance. Another theory could be that the person who made the design in this particular Mola was evil and that offended the Lord. Before they threw it in the trash they ripped up the Mola. They felt like two **"nut cases"** ripping up this beautiful piece of art, but they did not want anyone else picking it up out of the trash and putting it up on their walls.

Joshua said to the people, "He is a holy God. He is jealous God."
Josh. 24:19

* * *

Sanctity: God does not like to share His people with sin. This was precisely the reason He sent His only Son to cleanse us from transgressions. Defilement makes it difficult for God to protect us. Abominable things can rob us from our blessings.

Pam realized, keeping junk files was not pleasing to the Lord, not when she and her friend were trying to write a book to honor Him.

In the Bible when Joshua sent 3,000 troops to annihilate Ai, it was surprising that they were defeated and forced to retreat. Ai was a small place. The Israeli army had sufficient manpower to utterly destroy the City. When Joshua asked the Lord about what had happened, the Lord answered, **"I told you I wanted the entire city of Jericho destroyed, but instead your people have stolen and hidden goods for themselves."** God instructed Joshua to destroy the items and rid themselves of the guilty party if they ever wanted to win another battle again. Josh. 7:1-26

"Get up, sanctify the people, and say, sanctify yourselves for tomorrow, because thus says the Lord God of Israel: "There is an accursed thing in your midst, O Israel; you cannot stand before your enemies until you take away the accursed thing from among you." Josh. 7:13

* * *

I know of a person to whom Our Lord wished to show what a soul was like when it committed mortal sin.
That person says that if people could understand this, she thinks they would find it impossible to sin at all, and, rather than meet occasions of sin, would put themselves to greatest trouble imaginable. For, just as all the streamlets that flow from a clear spring are clear as the spring itself, so the works of the soul in grace are pleasing in the eyes both of God and of men, since they proceed from this spring of life, in which the soul is as a tree planted. It would give no shade and yield no fruit if it proceeded not thence, for the spring sustains it and prevents it from drying up and causes it to produce good fruit.

Teresa of Avila

Being committed to the Lord means sanctification. Mother Angelica, a cloistered nun devoted to prayer and working for the Lord says, **"We are all called to be Saints."** Even though her profession was mostly called to prayer, she says, **"Prayer takes many forms."** She is the one that started the Eternal Word Television Network. She knows what it is to be committed to work for the Lord. The Roman Catholic Church is an ancient Christian religious denomination operated and run by men. But, God chose this small, ill, stricken nun to begin a global telecommunication cable network. God works in mysterious ways.

It is mysterious that for some reason God chose Mother Angelica to start such an important operation instead of one of the men in this religious organization. This Italian woman was born with a birth defect; a weakness in her spine. One day in Canton, Ohio while she was cleaning and polishing the floors of a monastery with a power machine that had hand controls and a rotary brush, the machine spun out of control and hit exactly that place in her spine that was weak. After two years of terrible pain, surgery was recommended with the great risk of Mother Angelica not walking again. She promised the Lord that if she walked again she would build a monastery in the South. The operation was a success and left her with the necessity of having to wear a back brace and a leg brace. She kept her promise, with the permission of her mother superior and five nuns. They arrived at Birmingham, Alabama with plans to build a monastery. When the news begin to spread about these nuns who wanted to build a building, people began to drop by to see them, sometimes out of curiosity, since only 2 percent of the population were Catholic; however, most of them wanted to help. Before long they were receiving help from the Catholic community, other Christian communities and Jewish congregations.

Commit your way to the Lord, Trust also in Him, And He shall bring it to pass. He shall bring forth your righteousness as the light, And your justice as the noonday. Rest in the Lord, and wait patiently for Him. Ps. 37:5-7

The building of the monastery was completed, and by the 1970s the community had grown to twelve nuns. For their upkeep, the nuns sold booklets with the message of God all over the world. Little did the nuns know what God had planned for them. They would do broadcast interviews promoting their books. When they did an interview in Chicago, which was when Mother Angelica decided they needed a television station. At first she thought it was a ridiculous idea, but, by then, she had learned to accept crazy- sounding ideas. God's provision is large according to our faith and willingness to obey, she says, **"Be careful not to limit God's blessings by lack of faith."**

"And I will add to your days fifteen years, I will deliver you and this city from the hand of the king of Assyria; and I will defend this city for My own sake." 2 Kin. 20:6

This information was obtained from the book called Answers Not Promises by Mother M. Angelica with Christine Allison. Mother Angelica is not out to convert but to clarify. Her practical faith shows us to be so. These are a couple of her answers, not promises. She says,

"Answers don't really come in magic formulas or neat prescriptions. In fact, sometimes the truth seems ridiculous, but unless we are willing to do the ridiculous, God won't do the miraculous."

WHY WON'T HE SPEAK UP?

If our Mother Angelica Live Show is any indication, of one of the things that bugs people most about God is that He is always silent. You wouldn't believe how many people call in to complain about it. "How am I supposed to believe in someone Who never speaks to me?" "How do I know if He's heard my prayer?" "Why won't God just come right out and tell me the answers to my problems?" they ask. Without trying to be funny, I tell them to *listen.* That's a tough notion, because we usually presume that silence means absence. We figure that since we have voices, then

God must have a louder Voice! This is a good example of how our finite mind can get us into a lot of trouble.

* * *

This reminds Anton about Beth Moore, a great Evangelist. She said in one of her broadcast speeches that one of her children had once mentioned to her **"But, mom, when God speaks to me, He sounds just like me."** Like the saying says **"out of the mouth of babes,"** and this is actually in the Bible,

But when the chief priests and scribes saw the wonderful things that He did, and the children crying out in the temple and saying, "Hosanna to the Son of David!" they were indignant and said to Him, Do you hear what these are saying?" And Jesus said to them, "Yes. Have you never read, out of the mouth of babes and nursing infants You have perfected praise?" Matt. 21:15-16

* * *

Anton and Pam slowly began working; they felt that at every turn, life was keeping them from doing God's work. Pam has severe arthritis, but in spite of everything, it has been a wonderful and an exciting experience to get together. Together they are trying to learn, absorb and comprehend all the information of the Lord that marvels the mind. They feel the time they spend together is both inspirational and motivational. They would get together every Monday and work for two hours.

One of the first things Pam did was to buy a Bible for Anton, so she could compare the vibrations she was receiving with scripture. Trying to understand the language in the original King James Version is usually too difficult for most people, so she picked out a simpler English Version of a Bible. It was broken down into daily readings from the Old Testament, New Testament, Psalms and Proverbs.

"Beware of false prophets, who come to you in sheep's clothing, but inwardly they are ravenous wolves." Matt. 7:15

Anton was appreciative and thought, **"I will read it every night, and within a year I will know the Bible."** This was too good to be true. When she began reading this Bible, she noticed it was very negative, but since she was not familiar with scripture, she did not pay much attention to the negativity. She did notice, however, that the very next day she had a terrible day. Sometimes we have days when everything that can go wrong does go wrong. She did not want to associate her bad luck with reading the Bible, but, then the fallowing day was just as bad. She started to have doubts about the vibrations. Perhaps they were not from the Lord, or the enemy was upset she was reading the Bible. The mind can be deceiving, precisely the reason to be close to the Lord. He can help us discern what is good and what is bad. After having an awful week, she asked the Holy Spirit, **"What in the world is going on? Is God not pleased that I am making an effort to read the Bible?"** The vibrations of the Spirit answered, **"The Bible you were reading this past week was not interpreted the way God intended it to be."** She was astonished that He waited until she asked. This is how respectful He is, although He had taken His protection away from her to get her attention.

"You will know them by their fruits. Do men gather grapes from thornbushes or figs from thistles? Even so, every good tree bears good fruit, but a bad tree bears bad fruit." Matt. 7:16-17

We will only be happy in our reading of the Bible when we dare to approach it as the means by which God really speaks to us, the God who loves us and will not leave us with our questions unanswered.

Dietrich Bonhoeffer

Bible

The whole Bible is God's inspired word and the history of God's chosen people, through whom Jesus was born. It records the beginning of Christianity.

All Scripture is given by inspiration of God, and is profitable for doctrine, for reproof, for correction, for instruction in righteousness. 2 Tim. 3:16

When a person or even Bible scholars take the liberty of translating the Bible, they must be very careful because they risk the use of improper translation of the actual language or message God intended. God is not pleased for His people to be exposed to incorrect translations of His word. If Bibles and religious books are not protected and sanctioned by God, then evil can penetrate through the words, misleading us and weakening our faith in God's actual word. We would miss the true message and the plan He has for our life. It is an abomination to God when authors twist words and mislead Christians to false doctrine.

Adam and Eve were commanded by God not to eat of the tree of knowledge of good and evil. They were told,

"For in the day that you eat of it you shall surely die." Gen. 2:17

They did not think anything would happen. Just like we do not believe that events that are in the Bible can probably happen today. Of course, judgment came upon them with the factor of death.

Prophets: It is intriguing how these books of the Bible were composed by prophets who were guided by revelations and their knowledge shared for future generations. These people treated their revelations with great-caution and reverence. All scripture was written with profound responsibility, a declaration of divine inspiration with an indication of spiritual guidance. Remarkable indeed is the way it all came about, how intricate God's plan was to get this **Holy Book** out, against great odds. The Bible is an amazing collection of laws, history, saga, poetry, prophecies, biographies and theology. It is a story of God's love and pursuit of the human race.

To Him who loved us and washed us from our sins in His own blood. And has made us kings and priests to His God and Father, to Him be glory and dominion forever and ever. Amen.
Rev. 1:5-6

Holy Scripture and other writings are not as a Prerequisite to letting God speak through a text or verse of the Bible. Accurate, academic dissection of the material was not the primary aim of being with the word. Instead the approach was to sit quietly in the presence of God and with open heart and mind to wait until the text touched a deep place within and invited the listener into conversation with its Author.

Elizabeth J. Canham

* * *

The word Bible means book in Greek, but actually it is not one book, but several. It was written by many writers who were inspired by the word of the Lord. It took several centuries to collect all the different writings composed about the history of the Jewish people, later came the Christian scriptures. All this occurred in different stages, the first being the oral accounts of Hebrew people from Egypt. Stage two was writing and stage three was reproduction and transmission of handmade manuscripts. The Jewish religious people circulated as many manuscripts as they could. Imagine the passion and faith these people must have had in their hearts to be able to circulate the manuscripts so people could obtain the information about the true God. In the early biblical times there were no printing presses to make this job easier.

Stage four was putting prophecies in special categories and using them for public worship. Christians have always considered the Old Testament as the authoritative word of the Lord, just as the Jews believed. Stage five consisted of collecting this authoritative information on a wider range. The first five books of the Old Testament were recognized as the authoritative word of the Lord by around 400.B.C.E. and the rest the Hebrew Scriptures stood well by 100.C.E. The final stage is the association between Hebrew scripture and Christian scripture. Christians' writings were added to the Old Testament: the Synoptic Gospels--Matthew, Mark, Luke and John. Then the rest of the New Testament contained the Epistles, such as, the works of Paul, Peter, John, Titus, James and Jude. Twenty seven books were added until the fourth Century.

Then Jeremiah called Baruch the son of Neriah; and Baruch wrote on a scroll of a book, at the instructions of Jeremiah, all the words of the Lord which He had spoken to him. Jer. 36:4

The first circulation of the Bible was written in Hebrew, with a few Aramaic passages. The New Testament was written in Greek, which was the most popular language in the Roman Empire in the first century. Later it was translated in Latin, then into other popular languages-Hebrew, Coptic, Armenian, and others. This practice continues today.

Christians always considered the two sets of scripture essential for our spiritual growth. The Jewish people lived with only Hebrew Scriptures of the Old Testament for centuries. Both Jews and Christians feel this is the word of God free of human error. For God inspired the prophets with infallible words of information by revelation. They were appointed people with authority and guidance of the Almighty.

Knowing the history of the Bible helps understand the compellability, responsibility and authority somebody must have for the Bible to be translated into any language. Anton learned her lesson with the Bible Pam gave to her, which was written in simple English for the lay person. But, the Bible does not have to be translated into any simple language, because God does not consider any of His children to be simple minded. There is a reason why Jesus talked in parables. He knew that with the comforter, which is the Holy Spirit in us we would **understand His word.**

The Purpose of Parables

Then the disciples asked Him, saying, "What does this parable mean?" And He said, "To you it has been given to know the mysteries of the kingdom of God, but the rest it is given in parables, that 'seeing they may not see, And hearing they may not understand.'
Luke 8:9

Understanding the Bible does not involve intellect, only faith and the discipline to the will of God. These actions activate the presence of the Holy Spirit in a powerful way. The Holy Spirit helps us with spiritual knowledge and we see everything clearly without confusion. Requesting help from the Holy Spirit is a must to understand scripture. He will come to our aid and assist us. This Spirit of God will illuminate our minds and give vitality to the word of the Bible. We need for the word to be alive so it can penetrate **our hearts.**

For the word of God is living and powerful, and sharper than any two-edged sword, piercing even to the division of the soul and spirit.
Heb. 4:12

"It is the Spirit who gives life; the flesh profits nothing. The words that I speak to you are spirit, and they are life.
John 6:63

In the heart is where God can transcend us into an entire different existence; meaning we begin living more in the spirit realm than in the physical realm. In spirit is where we comprehend the word of the Lord.

Where the Spirit does not open the Scripture, the Scripture is not understood

even though it is rely on.

Martin Luther

Footnotes for the scriptures of the Bible are recommended. We can read the Bible and if there is any doubt about understanding the scripture, then we read the footnotes. This will help us identify our own understanding and will result in our own **personal revelation.**

* * *

Anton felt terrible having to tell her friend that her gift was not good, that this particular Bible was not satisfactory to God and was not of any value. She did not want to hurt her feelings, but Pam would ask her questions about the Bible. She had given her the Bible with the best intentions. Anton felt apologetic that the Holy Spirit had ruled it ineffectual for her to read. She did not want to offend Pam. She prayed to God to give her the courage and the proper words to tell her what the Holy Spirit' vibrations had said about this particular Bible. To her surprise, Pam understood.

Pam told Anton that she had being watching John Hagee's Sunday sermon. Pastor Hagee told his viewing audience about a new Bible that he was offering, which included some of his sermons that he had accumulated over the years. He had included them in the New King James Bible. He also used Bible study material from Porter L. Barrington. Not one word from the NKJV had been changed. Pam suggested this Bible. Perhaps the study guides and all the additional information in this Bible would help Anton to understand the Word of God as He wanted her to understand. God does not want anyone else talking to us but Himself. We must pray to God not to allow anyone else to speak to our heart, mind and soul. Jesus said,

"And I will pray to the Father, and He will give you another Helper, that He may abide with you forever. The Spirit of truth, whom the world cannot receive, because it neither sees Him nor knows Him; but you know Him, for He

dwells with you and will be in you."
John 14:16-17

Anton did buy the Bible that Pastor John Hagee put together using the N.K.J. Bible. She did ask the Holy Spirit's permission first, and it has been of great help.

* * *

The King James Bible was prepared and published in the year 1611. It is still used after more than 390 years in preference to any other version by the English-speaking Protestants for public and personal use. Some information on the N.K.J.V. Bible was obtained from the New International Bible Dictionary, J.D. Douglas Revising Editor and Merrill C. Tenney General Editor.

King James (Authorized) Version. When Elizabeth died in 1603, the crown passed to James 1, who had been king of Scotland for thirty six years as James V1. Several months after he ascended the throne of England he called a conference of bishops and Puritan clergy to harmonize the differences that existed in the church. At this conference Dr. John Reynolds, President of Corpus Christi College, Oxford, a leader of the Puritan party in the Church of England, suggested that a new translation of the Bible be made to replace the Bishops' Bible, which many people found unacceptable. The proposal pleased the King, who violently disliked the Geneva Bible; a resolution was passed to produce a new translation of the Bible from the original Hebrew and Greek, without any marginal notes, for the use of all the churches in England.

Of course, there are other wonderful different versions of the Bible. It would be impossible to name them all in this book. It just happened that Anton's first Bible was the New King James Version. She will be reading other versions, with time, so she can compare the full meaning of a verse, since the original Bible was written with 11,280 Hebrew, Aramaic and Greek words. The standard versions in English translations use only around 6,000 words. We can see the importance of what the Holy Spirit has to do for the full understanding of God's word. He has to fill the gaps of what was left out through the translations for us to appreciate the full meaning of the word. We must first consider what the passage meant in the day and age of the author before we try to understand the message for us in today's culture and apply it to our lives. God does not ever expect us to memorize chapter and verse of passages in the Bible. We are not going to be judged on memory, or on how we memorize chapter and verse, but instead on how we lived the word. We must try to live ethically and restrain ourselves from what is evil and live according to the will of God. There are some Christians that think if Christ lives in us there is no restraint, because we are naturally and automatically good. That is deceiving ourselves, because as long as we are in the flesh and in this world there will be temptations, good against evil. It is warfare and a struggle to stay in the Spirit. This is precisely the reason to remain in the word and read the Bible. This will help to prevent unpleasant thoughts from penetrating our subconscious which can eventually destroy our lives. Throughout the Bible God reveals truths about how humans can go wrong, but Christian human conduct will prevail through God's redemption and grace. The ultimate solution is Jesus Christ and His teachings of the **renewal of His followers.**

"However, when He, the Spirit of truth, has come, He will guide you into all truth; for He will not speak on His own authority, but whatever He hears He will speak; and He will tell you things to come." John 16:13

THE BIBLE IS RECOGNIZED BY

CHRISTIAN CHURCHES AS THE REVELATION

OF PROPHETS INSPIRED BY THE WORD OF GOD,

REVEALING THE INSPIRATIONS HE HAS FOR MANKIND.

* * *

I learn to listen while I read. Sometimes I would hear nothing except the words of my reading. More often, I was simply conscious that the passages were entering my mind and heart and becoming part of me. But increasingly there were times when some aspects of what I was reading came home to me with such sudden strength and clarity that I was left with no doubt that God had something to say not just to the psalmist, the prophet, or the disciple--but to me.

Avery Brooke

Your testimonies are wonderful; therefore my soul keeps them. The entrance of Your words gives light; It gives understanding to the simple. I opened my mouth and panted, For I longed for Your commandments. Look upon me and be merciful to me, As Your custom is toward those who love Your name. Direct my steps by Your word, And let no iniquity have dominion over me. Redeem me from the oppression of man, That I may keep Your precepts, Make Your face shine upon Your servant. Ps. 119:129-135

Chapter 5

BAPTISM

This sacrament provides a reality beyond our senses, a mystery involving spiritual understanding and a binding toward God.

"The time is fulfilled, and the kingdom of God is at hand. Repent, and believe in the gospel." Mark 1:15

The use of water in baptism signifies cleansing and regeneration. We are clean of sin through the blood of Christ and partakers of the mystery of dying to sin and being raised to a new life through the resurrection of Christ's death. This ritual is necessary for the inner change in the spiritual. We are sharing common origin (kinship by adoption) an affiliation to a community that is the body of Christ. There has to be an outward decision; in other words, we have to decide to accept this spiritual inward act in order to activate it in our soul and spirit. The important and main decision is to receive this sacrament because this physical event is marked by a spiritual reality. Perhaps, we will not hold in our memory the moment of our decision to actually accept this experience. But nevertheless, the experience will become legally valid at the moment we accept Jesus as our Lord and savior. When we accept being baptized in the name of the Father, of the Son and of the Holy Spirit, our life will change forever. We are a new creature in Christ, born again in the spirit inheriting the Holy Spirit, because this Spirit is part of the Holy Trinity. He is the helper that makes all things possible and for us to be with the Son and the Father available to all believers. Jesus said,

"At that day you will know that I am in My Father, and you in Me and I in you. He who has My commandments and keeps them, it is he who loves Me. And he who loves Me will be loved by My Father, and I will love him and manifest Myself to him." John 14:20-21

* * *

Birth was the subject of discourse between the Lord Jesus and Nicodemus, a Pharisee. Nicodemus began by saying, **"Rabbi, we know that you are a teacher come from God, for no man can do these signs that You do unless God is with him."** Jesus knows all men's hearts and minds. This prompted Jesus to raise the issue of spiritual birth ignoring Nicodemus's complimentary remarks.

Jesus answered and said to him, "Most assuredly, I say to you, unless one is born again he cannot see the kingdom of God." Nicodemus said to Him, "How can a man be born when he is old? Can he enter a second time into his mother's womb and be born?" Jesus answered, "Most assuredly, I say to you, unless one is born of water and the Spirit, he can not enter the kingdom of God. That which is born of flesh is flesh, and that which is born of spirit is spirit." John 3:3-6

Jesus knew this devoutly religious man was not spiritual, so he was not going to understand. Nicodemus received a supernatural insight to his natural question, but unless we are born of the Spirit we will not be able to understand supernatural insights.

It is difficult to understand this concept of being born again through our five senses. Trying to reason this phenomenon of birth with our intellect will logically be rejected. We need to use our simplistic character judgment which is our imagination. This is where our creativity is, the part of our mind where our thoughts are formed. Using our imagination will intuitively help us arrive at the logic of our existence. Because God communicates with us through our thoughts, He helps us to form, create and visualize images and ideas that will materialize in physical form, becoming real. Idealizing and retaining this information from our thoughts that we are born again through the Spirit, will consciously create an act of creative semblance in reality of our baptism. First we are creatures of the flesh being born from the flesh. Through baptism we are born through the spirit, new creatures in Christ, being adopted by God the Father that is all Spirit.

You received the Spirit of adoption by whom we cry out. "Abba, Father." Not only that, but we also have the first fruits of the Spirit, even ourselves groan within ourselves, eagerly waiting for the adoption, the redemption of our body. Rom. 8:15, 23

The New Testament writers speak as if Christ's achievement in rising from the dead was the first event of its kind in the whole history of the universe. He is the 'first fruits', 'the pioneer of life.' He has opened a door that has been locked since the death of the first man. He has met, fought, and beaten the King of Death. Everything is different because He has done so. This is the beginning of the New Creation: a new chapter in cosmic history has opened.

C.S. Lewis

It is critical to comprehend the disposition and condition of us humans; we are beings of both spirit and body. Physical ritual procedures are essential for a glorious restoration of our sinful life. The spiritual world is continuously interchanging with the physical world, complimenting each other. Born again gives us the right to enjoy both worlds. **"We have the best of both worlds,"** aligning ourselves with the greatest power of the universe. It is truly amazing to our senses when we can envision this act of birth through the Spirit and contemplate it in our mind. Becoming children of God gives us the attribution of the Holy Spirit's exotic works. It is actually God's love working in a remarkable way. But our imagination, visualization and contemplation has to be our primary factor in understanding this extraordinary, prophetic and significant happening.

Imagination is the capacity to make connection between the visible and the invisible, between heaven and earth, between present and past, between present and future. For Christians, whose largest investment is in the invisible, the imagination is indispensable, for it is only by means of imagination that we see reality whole, in context.

Eugene H. Peterson

* * *

The apostle Paul wrote to a church that he had founded in the early part of his ministry. Paul's authorship of the letter is scarcely doubted by anyone.

There is one glory of the sun, another glory of the moon, and another glory of the stars; for one star differs from another star in glory. So also is the resurrection of the dead. The body is sown in corruption, it is raised in incorruption. It is sown in dishonor, it is raised in glory. It is sown in weakness, it is raised in power. It is sown in a natural body, it is raised a spiritual body. There is a natural body, and there is a spiritual body .And so it is written, "The first man Adam became a living being." The last Adam became a life-giving Spirit. However, the spiritual is not the first, but the natural, and afterward the spiritual. The first man was of the earth, made of dust; the second Man is the Lord from heaven. As was the man of dust, so also are those who are made of dust, and as is the heavenly Man, so also those who are heavenly. And as we have born the image of the man of dust, we shall also bear the image of the heavenly Man. 1 Cor.15:41-49

Paul knew that the symbol of baptism says it all; being buried with Christ and raised with Christ means we are now to live as new, born-again people.

Buried with Him in baptism, in which you also were raised with Him through faith in the working of God, who raised Him from the dead. Col. 2:12

**What does such baptizing with water signify?
It signifies that the old Adam in us is to be drowned
by daily sorrow and repentance, and perish with all
sins and evil lust; and the new man should daily come
forth again and rise, who shall live before God in
righteousness and purity.**

Martin Luther

If some believers have not been baptized, it is our Christian duty to recommend and suggest this sacrament. They must be introduced to this mystery of having their sins nailed to the Cross, proclaiming victory in the power of Jesus' resurrection and living as born-again Christians.

BAPTISM BECOMES CONSUMMATED WHEN

WE BELIEVE WHAT THE SACRAMENT REPRESENTS.

**"A sacrament is a corporeal or material
element set before the senses without, representing
by similitude and signifying by institution and
containing by sanctification some invisible
and spiritual grace."**

Hugh of Saint Victor

* * *

Commission: Baptism is also a commission to be active in winning the lost.

"For the Son of Man has come to save that which was lost." Matt. 18:11

Jesus commanded us to make disciples of all nations, beginning with our own home and continuing to move outward until eventually, as a church, we reach the nations of the world. Jesus said to the disciples,

"All authority has been given to me in heaven and on earth. Go therefore and make disciples of all nations, baptizing them in the name of the Father and of the Son and of the Holy Spirit, teaching them to observe all things that I have commanded you; And lo, I am with you always, even to the end of the age." Matt. 28:18

Observe, that Jesus did not just command the disciples to inform people of what He had commanded, but said **"Baptize them"** because it is the first and most important step toward **growing in grace**.

To whom pertain the adoption, the glory, the covenants, the giving of the law, the service of God, and the promises. Rom. 9:4

Therefore Triumphs in Trouble

Therefore having been justified by faith we have peace with God through our Lord Jesus Christ, through whom also we have access by faith into this grace in which we stand, and rejoice in hope of the glory of God. And not only that, but we also glory in tribulations, knowing that tribulations produce perseverance; and perseverance, character; and character, hope. Now hope does not disappoint, because the love of God has been poured out in our hearts by the Holy Spirit who was given to us. Rom. 5:1-5

* * *

The promise: We are also heirs of God's assurance of His presence within us. Understanding God's promise is inheriting God's kingdom and eternal life. God's kingdom will give us the wisdom of the whole understanding of the equation of our existence. It will give us the realization of being sensible with the laws and principles that God has established on earth for the preservation of mankind. Understanding God's divine activity with His creation will assist us with our expectations and make us realistic about our evolution. When we appreciate and value the whole equation and evolution of Christian life, we will experience contentment and richness (substance) in our lives.

"Most assuredly, I say to you, he who believes in Me has everlasting life. I am the bread of life." John 6:47-48

THE PROMISE

THERE IS NO TRANSLATION FOR THE WORD PROMISE IN HEBREW, "WORD," "SPEAK" AND "SAY" ARE USED INSTEAD. HOWEVER, IN THE NEW TESTAMENT WE CAN INTERPRET THE WORD PROMISE IN A LOGICAL WAY, THAT GOD PROMISES TO VIST HIS CHILDREN THROUGH JESUS' SACRIFICIAL ACT. NOW GOD CAN SPEAK TO US THROUGH HIS SON'S PROMISE THAT HE WOULD PRAY TO GOD TO SEND US ANOTHER HELPER THAT WOULD ABIDE IN US, THE HOLY SPIRIT. GOD SPEAKS TO US, WHICH IS THE PROMISE AND WITH THE PROMISE COMES MANY BLESSINGS.

* * *

Christians' covenant: Our covenant with God is through Jesus, and the practice of baptism is the confirmation. Baptism also signifies we are resurrected with Him to inherit all of God's riches, to fulfill God's purpose. We are justified (acceptable) by our faith. Our faith is accountable for righteousness (to be right with God) which means to do His will and live by His word.

"He who believes in Me, believes not in Me but in Him who sent Me. And he who sees Me sees Him who sent Me. I have come as a light into the world, that whoever believes in Me should not abide in darkness."
John 12:44-46

JESUS THE MEDIATOR OF THE NEW COVENANT.

"For I will be merciful to their unrighteousness and their sins and their lawless deeds I will remember no more" In that He says, "A new covenant." Heb. *8:12-13*

* * *

Abraham's covenant: We Christians also have received patriarchs from Abraham, who was a religious leader of Hebrew people and ancestor of God's human race. In the New Testament we have Mary, Joseph and Jesus, the first family of Christendom. They also came from Abraham's tree. We Christians are a redeemed race. Through Christ we inherit the righteousness of God. By faith we are partakers of His divine nature.

Circumcision signified the confirmation of the covenant God made with Abraham. Thus, his descendants would inherit God's promise, which is God's grace, the source that will bring forth God's riches. They will walk in His presence, enjoying His sufficient supply, which means His government and authority will supply whatever they need. They did not rely on man's government or in their own sufficiency and power, but in the All-Sufficient, the Almighty.

There was conflict over circumcision among certain men and Pharisees. They taught that unless you are circumcised, you are not a child of God and cannot be saved. The apostles and the elders of the church came together regarding this matter, for the conversion of the **Gentiles.**

And when there had been much dispute, Peter rose up and said to them: "Men and brethren, you know that a good while ago God chose

among us, that by my mouth the Gentiles should hear the word of the gospel and believe. "So God, knows the heart, acknowledged them by giving them the Holy Spirit, just as He did to us, and made no distinction between us and them, purifying their heart by faith."
Acts 15:7-9

"But we believe that through the grace of our Lord Jesus Christ we shall be saved in the same manner as they." Acts 15:11

For the promise that he would be the heir of the world was not to Abraham or to his seed through the law, but through the righteousness of faith. Rom. 4:13

With these quotations one might think that faith covers the whole concept of believing, but if we had not sinned, perhaps no formal agreement would be necessary. Unfortunately, we have original sin, making covenant implicit in our relationship with the Lord. Abraham's covenant with God was for the male to be circumcised, making his descendents part of the community of God's people. The Christians' covenant through Jesus Christ has to be a formal act which is baptism. It is planned for the outpouring of the Holy Spirit and expressing our faith into love that enacts grace towards the community of the **Church.**

The circumcision in the Old Testament not only represents an outward transformation, but an inward transformation of the heart in the Spirit. This means to put off the flesh so that self and the old person become children of God. The epistle of Paul mentions,

But he is a Jew who is one inwardly; and circumcision is that of the heart, in the Spirit, not in the letter; whose praise is not from men but from God. Rom. 2:29

God selected Abraham to be the Father of a great multitude, because God needs more than one exalted person. He needs a multitude to fulfill his eternal purpose. He is the Godhead of the church. **We are His family.**

We humans are physical beings; however, we are also spiritual beings who need help from God that is all Spirit. He is our source and creator, the reason we seek the reality of His existence and want Him to be accessible. Although faith is essential for our communication, we need more of a sense of divine grace. We also require the fullness of the Holy Spirit in order to grasp beyond our reach, appreciating the reality of the mystery in our senses. This helps us function well in both areas of the spectrum, the physical and spiritual realm. We need to walk in the Lord's presence, because physical elements are not going to provide us with spiritual satisfaction and God's blessings. This is the reason for the practice of the ritual act of covenant. Covenant is a binding pact to be committed to each other and establishes a relationship.

GOD DOES NOT REVEAL HIMSELF TO HIS

CURIOUS CHILDREN, BUT TO THE OBEDIENT.

If we read Genesis, chapter sixteen, we will notice that Sarah was not blessed with a child until Abraham was circumcised, even though Sarah was eighty years old and Abraham one hundred. In fact, they both thought it was humorous that somebody at that age would have a child. This is an example of how nothing is impossible for God. He patiently waited until they both relied on His strength and walked in His presence. God waited until they accepted and rejoiced in His economy (efficiency) and the plan He had for them, which is essential in order to receive His blessings. He changed their names, from Abram to Abraham, meaning father of a multitude, and Sarah also, meaning princess. The reason for changing their names was to enlarge and to broaden them, because now they were father and mother of all nations. They named their child Isaac, meaning laughter, because of how they thought it was humorous to have a child at their age. God's plan was for this couple to be an example for the rest of humanity.

God's promise was granted through faith, because even though this couple thought the promise was humorous, they did believe it would come to pass. Paul wrote on the importance of the righteousness of faith,

For if those who are of the law are heirs, faith is made void and the promise made of no effect. Rom. *4:14*

Faith is a vibrant and courageous confidence in God's grace. It is so sure and certain that believers would stake their lives on God's grace a thousand times. This confidence makes people joyful, bold, and happy in their relationship with God and with other people.

Martin Luther

By faith we understand that the worlds were framed by the word of God, so that the things which are seen were not made of things which are visible. Heb. *11:3*

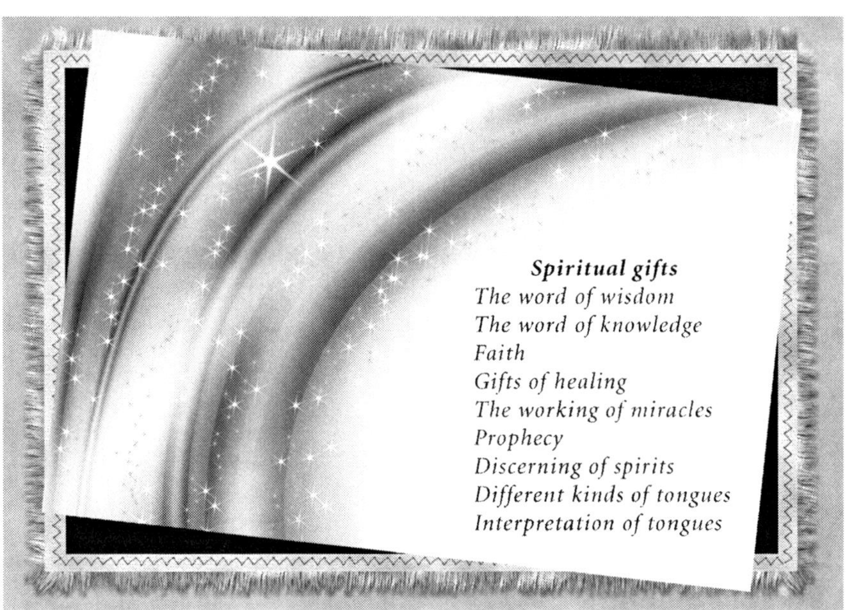

Spiritual gifts
The word of wisdom
The word of knowledge
Faith
Gifts of healing
The working of miracles
Prophecy
Discerning of spirits
Different kinds of tongues
Interpretation of tongues

O Lord, You are the portion of my inheritance and my cup; You maintain my lot. The lines have fallen to me in pleasant places; Yes I have a good inheritance. I will bless the Lord who has given me counsel; My heart also instructs me in the night seasons. I have set the Lord always before me; Because He is at my right hand I shall not be moved. Therefore my heart is glad, and my glory rejoices; My flesh also will rest in hope. Ps. 16:5-9

Holy Communion

Through Holy Communion we are reconciled with God, made with God. We are free to be in fellowship with God.

By that will we have been sanctified through the offering of the body of Jesus Christ once for all. Heb. 10:10

We all know how important the sacrament of baptism is. Some Christians baptize their child when he or she is an infant. They want to make sure their child receives this sacrament. But, what we are not aware of is the significance of the Holy Communion. When Anton started to address baptism, the Holy Spirit's vibrations instructed her to make sure to also give information about Holy Communion. She was puzzled, because she did not think communion was that important. The minute He mentioned this sacrament she remembered the verse that Jesus said.

"This is my body which is given for you: do this in remembrance of Me." Luke 22:19

It is difficult to be knowledgeable about all the verses in the Bible. However, she knew this one, and it caught her by surprise that the Holy Spirit would direct her to address Holy Communion. She thought, as Christians we already have Christ in our heart, so we do not have to take Communion to remember Him. The Holy Spirit, knowing her mind, responded, **"Holy Communion takes away sins."**

Jesus Institutes the Lord's Supper

And as they were eating, Jesus took bread, blessed and broke it, and gave it to the disciples and said, "Take, eat, this is My body." Then

He took the cup, and gave thanks, and gave it to them, saying, "Drink from it, all of you. For this is My blood of the new covenant, which is shed for many for the remission of sins." Matt. 26:26-28

* * *

The transfiguration that takes place in the Eucharist is beyond our comprehension as physical beings. But it does remind us of the glory of Jesus when He walked among us and of the sacrificial offering He made for us. This sacrament of Holy Communion means to take an **"oath"** of loyalty, a binding pledge as witnesses of Jesus sacrificial offering and as a word of promise to formally pledge our love. It is of great importance for the believer that receives this reconciliation to obtain a deeper understanding and knowledge of the mystery that involves this sacrament. It is the bread that came down from heaven, so we may eat of it for our redemption.

Christ ordained these sacraments of Baptism and Holy Communion as a means of conveying grace.

And of His fullness we have all received, and grace for grace. For the law was given through Moses, but grace and truth came through Jesus Christ. John 1:16-17

Faithful Christians should observe these ordinances to glorify the Lord by keeping God's temple (our body) clean of sin. The significance of taking Holy Communion means being justified, clean of sin. Our fallible mind and aimless conduct inherited from our parents are being redeemed and purified like silver and gold. This is done with the blood of Christ as the lamb without blemish and without original sin, as He was conceived by the Holy Spirit. We are being forgiven again and again. Of course, God knows our degenerate minds, and we cannot fool the infallible mind of God. The Lord is patient. He is capable of waiting without becoming annoyed or upset until we are sincere about our repentance. This is the reason for communion, to have the opportunity of His power to provide salvation for everyone who believes. Redemption begins with thoughts of repentance with faith in our mind. The apostle Peter talks of having faith in Jesus and redemption to perfect soundness of mind through repentance.

"Repent therefore and be converted, that your sins may be blotted out, so that times of refreshing may come from the presence of the Lord."
"To you first, God, having raised up His Servant Jesus, sent Him to bless you, in turning away every one of you from your iniquities."
Acts 3:19, 26

The Eucharist is a symbol of the inward cleansing by the blood of Jesus, so we can continue to grow in grace and knowledge of our Lord and Savior. We must not forget the significance of our baptism, which was an ordinance (law of religious ceremony) a public entrance into the church (body of Christ). The assembly of believers' responsibility is to keep the newness of church through our repentance. Our spiritual birth produces a soul that will never die, but the desires of our flesh are problematic for every Christian and will continue to be until our death. Nevertheless, we can be victorious over the old nature through the power of the indwelling **Holy Spirit.**

The sacraments presuppose that God has met us in history and that this meeting calls us to regular recollection and reenactment in order to experience God's real presence in the midst. The grace of God is offered in and through these sacraments in a way that we cannot grasp by our own moral efforts grace is being offered and, by faith, communicated to the believer in baptism and Holy Communion by Christ's own ordinance. They are means of grace Water, and bread, and wine express promises, not that we make to God but that God makes to us, to which we may respond in obedient faith. They are signs of God's mercy to us and of God's immediate presence in the midst. We are cleansed through water and fed through bread. We are brought into the community by baptism and sustained in community by communion.

Thomas C. Oden

* * *

Death and resurrection are the institutions of the Lord's Supper. When Jesus took the cup, blessed it and gave it to His disciples, He said,

"Drink from it all of you. But I say to you, I will not drink of this fruit of the vine from now on until that day when I drink it new with you in My Father's kingdom."
Matt. 26:27, 29

The apostle Paul claims that we proclaim Jesus' death as often as we eat this bread and drink this cup.

For as often as you eat this bread and drink this cup, you proclaim the Lord's death till He comes. 1 Cor. 11:26

Partaking in the Lord's Supper is taking the Eucharist, feast of thanksgiving. We repent of our sins and the blood of Jesus covers our guilt. As Christians we could also confess all our sins and repent in the name of Jesus and be forgiven, but it would be difficult to remember all of our sins. Holy Communion takes us back to our baptism and we are like a new born in spirit without sin. Of course, this sacrament should not be taken casually. We must examine our heart and make sure that we are truly in Christ that we are believers of this figurative representation of when God's Lamb bled and died on the cross for our sins. John the Baptist provides us with the answer,

"I baptize with water, but there stands One among you whom you do not know. It is He who, coming after me, is preferred before me, whose sandal strap I am not worthy to loose." the next day John saw Jesus coming toward him. and said, "Behold! The Lamb of God who takes away the sin of the world!" John 1:26-27, 29

* * *

The sacrament of Holy Communion has Jewish roots in their celebration of Passover. This ritual in the 1st century provided material elements; unleavened bread, lamb bones, wine and bitter herbs. The Passover celebration works with the same ideas as the Holy Communion. The death of the lamb was a sacrifice or offering for the cleansing and purification of their souls and to remind man how sinful and unfit they were to draw near the Holy God. They felt indebted to God because of their sins. The Day of Atonement was to cleanse them of their sins. The Lord's Supper was Christ's adaptation of the Jewish roots and the Passover feast for His church (Christians). The disciples asked Jesus,

"Where do You want us to go and prepare, that You may eat the Passover?" Mark 14:12

* * *

We are earthen vessels that need to be filled with the excellence of the power of God, believing that we are raised up with Jesus and He is with us. We contemplate the invisible that the outward man or woman perishes and the inward man or woman is being renewed and is concentrating on the event of communion as a real happening. Paul wrote in first Corinthians, which is an extremely important epistle because it concerns the period when the church was coming out of the darkness of paganism.

For since, in the wisdom of God, the world through wisdom did not know God, it pleased God through the foolishness of the message preached to save those that believe. Because the foolishness of God is wiser than men, and the weakness of God is stronger than men.
1 Cor. 1:21, 25

When we are baptized or take Communion we exercise the power of the Holy Spirit through redemption. He helps us with our eyes of faith to see the light of God and to see the power of the Father and Son in creation. He is responsible for the new birth of the believer and the helper that Jesus promised to the disciples after His ascension. The Holy Spirit reveals to Christians the deep things about God.

Now we have received, not the spirit of the world, but the Spirit who is from God, that we might know the things that have been freely given to us by God. 1 Cor. 2:12

* * *

There are some Christians who are blind and ignore the invitation of justification through Holy Communion. The reason is that we are misinformed about the significance. The need for Communion is a symbol of our failing and the perplexities that we suffer in our ascent to God. No one has been spared from failures in our life of faith, because we neglect to take the Bible at hand.

It seems there are Christians of different religious groups that have different concepts of what it is actually happening in this sacrament of the Holy Communion. The major belief in these groups is that the nature of Christ is present in the Eucharist.

Group one….. Believes in consubstantiation, which means the process of Jesus' body and blood coexists in the Eucharist consecrated at Communion with the natural elements of which the bread and wine are made.

Group two….. Believes in transubstantiation, the Eucharist becomes a substance of the body and blood of Jesus at consecration, but not in appearance.

Group three ….. Believes in the presence and the power of Jesus Christ that is present in the Eucharist (bread and wine), if you receive it with faith.

Group four….. Believes very strongly that the service of the Eucharist is honoring Jesus and remembering His sacrifice, but do not believe or associate it with His presence.

Group five….. Believes and finds the Eucharist to be a healing service emotionally and physically. Everything is possible for those who believe, like the woman that touched Jesus' garment.

For she said to herself, "If only I may touch His garment, I shall be made well." But Jesus turned around, and when He saw her He said, "Be of good cheers, daughter; your faith has made you well." Matt. 9:21-22

The last group….. Believes in the Saving Ordinance, as Anton does now, that through the Eucharist we find redemption and restoration. The reason this is possible is because Jesus' grace is in the bread and wine.

Humans are complicated creatures. Our beliefs are complicated and sometimes can be confusing, because of distinct differences in doctrines or patterns in the sacrament of Communion. One thing we all agree on is the fact that these sacraments of Baptism and Holy Communion were **"ordained"** by Jesus Christ.

GOD CAME INTO HUMAN HISTORY. HE

ENTERED TO FREE US AND MAKES US EQUAL

THROUGH HIS ONLY BEGOTTEN SON. BECAUSE IF

WE ARE HIS CHIDREN WE ARE LIKE HIM IN SPIRIT.

And the Word became flesh and dwelt among us, and we beheld His glory, the glory as the only begotten of the Father, full of grace and truth. John 1:14

Sin

The wisdom of the Christian is in forgiveness; Jesus has given it to us by making atonement for our sins.

Wash me thoroughly from my iniquity, And cleanse me from my sin. Behold, You desire truth in my inward parts, And in the hidden part You will make me to know wisdom. Ps. 51:2, 6

We are a sophisticated generation, but are still naïve when it comes to knowing everything about sin. The reason is because we do not have sufficient information about God. Restraining ourselves from not sinning is more than just a courtesy to God. Our human susceptibility rarely comprehends the consequences of disobedience and rebellion against God. Our physical nature and temperament blinds us to the seriousness of the problem about sin. We are dominated with temptations in the secular establishment. There is no evidence of quick gratification for us anxious Christians to choose goodness and kindness. We are an impatient generation and want results and rewards immediately for everything we do in this world. Analyzing the whole equation, it is quite astonishing that anybody does choose the **right path.**

Anton is still overwhelmed and surprised about how she arrived to this state of consciousness with the Holy Spirit. As mentioned before, it was pure coincidence, when she decided to pray the Lord's Prayer every night, without really being conscious of what she was doing. The prayer was actually asking for forgiveness every night for her sins, **"Forgive our trespasses as we forgive those who trespass against us."** It took more than a year of faithfully asking for forgiveness before the Lord showed His presence with a tender touch, and then another five years before she realized what it was. She thinks back humorously, **"It took longer than three hundred and sixty five nights of asking for**

forgiveness before the Lord cleaned me of sin. I must have really been dirty and stained."

DELIVERANCE AND RECONCILIATION

WITH GOD IS BEING CLEAN FROM SIN.

"For I am the Lord your God. You shall therefore consecrate yourselves, and you shall be holy; for I am holy." Lev. 11:44

AN UNWASHED SOUL, WILL

DEPRIVE US OF THE COMPANY OF GOD.

The Bible tells us that sin is more than psychological maladjustment or a breach of courtesy or breaking a promise. The Old Testament tells us that sin brings consequences and it can become a curse up to the fourth generation. Sin should never occur now because all we have to do is believe in Christ, repent and ask for forgiveness to be free of the stain of sin through the **blood of Jesus.**

God has made the fall of humankind and the existence of sin His issue. Through His love He has made forgiveness His issue too. God is always trying to preserve unity in His mystical body. He infuses us with the meaning of life through His mercy, goodness, acceptance, forgiveness and hope. One only needs to stay vigilant against the evil that oppresses and dehumanizes the body of Christ. We can protect our selves with God's strength, His unconditional love and the forgiveness of our sins. There are no psychological answers to the understanding of the fundamental uniqueness of how God protects us and His concern for the mystical body. Our theological knowledge does not understand the cosmic vision that God has for the salvation of the human race. Only when we accidentally confront our own mystery (communion with God) can we comprehend the strangeness of **"being here"** and understand our existence, our evolvement and **the plan He has for us.**

Amazing Grace
How sweet the sound, that saved a wretch like me! I once was lost, but now am found, was blind, but now I see.

John Newton

We are so finely interwoven with each other that it is impossible to understand where the origin of our sorrow began; for example, when somebody is diagnosed with lung cancer when that person never smoked cigarettes. In other words, this sickness came from somebody who sinned in the community of Christians. The distress and the wrong doing of a spirit will eventually affect the body of Christ. On the other hand, pain is a great equalizer, and the good virtue of souls is also an equalizer; they both bring balance to the ethical system of Christianity. Our sinful nature causes destruction and pain to all of us by disturbing the equilibrium of our association with the Lord. Paul reminds us of Jesus' love for the church, meaning the institution of Christians also referred to as **His body.**

Christ also loved the church and gave Himself for her, that He might sanctify and cleanse her with the washing of water by the word, that He might present her to Himself a glorious church, not having spot or wrinkle or any such thing, but that she should be holy and with out blemish. Eph. 5:25-27

* * *

God gave His highest ranking angel dominion over earth, but then this angel decided to rebel against Him. Whether it really happened like the prophets wrote in the Bible or it is a metaphor for how evil came into existence, we will never know. The idea here is that God has to live with our bad decisions. When Anton asked the Holy Spirit if the Devil existed, the only answer she got from the vibrations was, **"Evil does exist."**

You are of God, little children, and have overcome them, because He who is in you is greater than he who is in the world. 1 John 4:4

God had a monumentally clever plan to deceive this malevolent enemy and his evil ways. Because of the crucifixion of His Son, we are not helpless against this mythological creature that causes us to sin and have devastation and desperation in our lives. God uses pain and suffering to purify us; pain is a reality, but not the ultimate reality. God has invested us with the capacity to win this unceasing struggle. The love God has for the human species gives Him the responsibility to aid and help us with our every day struggles.

Affliction has a way of making us see each other in a special way. It helps us to get our values in perspective. Nobody can experience pain and suffering without becoming mature; compassionate Christians, **fit for God's love.**

This is my comfort in my affliction, for Your word has given me life. Ps. 119:50

AMONG ALL HUMAN EXPERIENCES PAIN IS THE

MOST EQUALIZING, IT BRINGS US THE PIVOTAL POINT

OF OUR EXISTENCE AND EVALUATES OUR PRIORITIES.

This quote does not mean to welcome or embrace pain, but we must respect and realize that we learn and grow from painful experiences left in our character. The pain and suffering of Jesus' crucifixion brought knowledge of God's laws.

Through Baptism Christians are all called to be ministers of God's word; therefore, He is the ultimate employer. He can use us as He chooses. Experiences of sorrow and pain are necessary because they are the strongest of emotions. These are essential emotional elements for the evolvement of caring in human beings. Our suffering has a spiritual mystical quality, concerning all of us in His body. We need to draw strength from the main source, which is God, and not become caught permanently dwelling in a life of pain.

"Behold, I stand at the door and knock. If anyone hears My voice and opens the door, I will come in to him and dine with him, and he with Me." Rev. 3:20

God demonstrated His love for mankind on the cross, to the point of becoming His Son as a sacrifice for sin, initiating the process of the reconciliation and being clean of sin. We are so fortunate now, because we can have union with God through Jesus. Before the crucifixion, the Holy Spirit was only for a few. Now we all can have access to the Holy Spirit through baptism and the belief that Jesus is our Lord and savior. The forgiveness of sins will keep us clean and give us the opportunity of eternal life. Nobody should conscientiously carry their sins now, when it is so uncomplicated to stay clean through repentance and the Holy Communion. Jesus already paid full price for our sins. God spoke the word and the word became flesh.

ONLY SOMEBODY DIVINE COULD

CARRY THE SINS OF THE WORLD.

The Body of Christ

With one body, namely His own, He blesses those who believe in Him as they partake of the holy mysteries and makes them members of the same body with Himself and with one another.

Cyril of Alexandria

We are constantly given the opportunity to enjoy God's grace even though we are descendents and offspring of carnal lust and tainted with original sin. He knows our hearts desire union with Him, for he is our creator and made in His image. Our spirit has the instinct of wanting to glorify Him and to join the blood line of becoming one of his children. But our spirit and soul struggle every day with our human insecurities, our desires of the flesh. Our flesh is prone to disobedience and carnal lust. Nevertheless, He will forgive us through His beloved Son and merciful grace. Our sins will be forgiven and forgotten if we come to Him in repentance.

THE ACT OF ASKING FOR

FORGIVENESS IS THE ACT OF REPENTANCE.

* * *

God's love is so merciful that he can turn a sinful horrific act into something completely the opposite. An example is the case of a noted televangelist, James Robinson His mother was a victim of rape. His entrance into the world was the product of a violent act. But this child grew up to be a Minister of God's word and a wonderful humanitarian. He helps many starving African children. When God cannot prevent our sinful nature to commit sin, he will meticulously try to change it for good. That is how God works.

* * *

We are living creatures who have evolved by a divine design, and who will eventually be through with our stay on earth. If we are fortunate, we will die of old age. It is unfortunate when somebody dies early and does not have the opportunity of a long life. God's blue print for the human body will stay behind when we die, so we cannot even begin to fathom or understand the concept of the soul. If God went through all that trouble to make the human body so incredibly intricate, and it will eventually disintegrate, then we cannot imagine what the soul must be made of. It will not be destroyed. God's evidence of His existence is in the human body and soul.

IT IS ESSENTIAL TO KEEP OUR SOUL

CLEAN JUST LIKE WE DO WITH OUR BODY.

In the Good News magazine, May-June, 2005, p.4, Mario *Seiglie* writes about the D.N.A, the tiny code of deoxyribonucleic acid that reproduces evolution. The article tells us how intricate the body is made.

It is difficult to fathom the amount of information in the human body's D.N.A. It is roughly equivalent to 12 sets of the Encyclopedia Britannica, an incredible 384 volumes worth of detailed information which could fill 48 feet of library shelves. The Psalm of David tells us how David had God's perfect knowledge of man.

"I will praise You, for I am fearfully and wonderfully made;
marvelous are Your works, and that my soul knows very well."
Ps. 139:14

A Christian

1. To be a Christian is to be awakened to the goodness and mercy of God through the proclamation of the gospel of Jesus Christ.

2. To be a Christian is to recognize that you are a sinner before God and need God's grace in order to be saved from the power and guilt of sin.

3. To be a Christian is to place your faith in Jesus Christ as Lord and Savior and to repent of sin.

4. To be a Christian is to intend to be Christ's faithful disciple, obeying His word and showing His love to your life's end.

5. To be a Christian is to belong to the church, Christ's body, and to participate actively and responsibly in its worship and mission.

Robert H. Ramey, Jr., and Ben Campbell Johnson

Chapter 6

COVENANT

Covenant is an act to please one whom one loves with the action of freedom. The one hope is to bring self into right relationship with God.

Christ came as High Priest and for the good things to come, He is the Mediator of the new covenant, by means of death, for the redemption of the transgressions under the first covenant. Heb. 9:11, 15

Anton was appreciative of the relationship with the Holy Spirit, but when He asked her to write a book about all the information she was accumulating, her first reaction was to refuse. She did not think that this could be possible and she said, **"I'm just an immigrant. I don't even speak the language very well."** But with God, nothing is impossible, and He prevails. She knew there are books on about any subject to help amateurs. When she arrived at the book store to try to find a book for dummies about How to Write a Novel, hoping this could help her execute the project. At the store she heard the whispers of the vibrations of the Holy Spirit that said, **"Get the one for idiots."** She responded, **"Gee thanks."** When she was reading the book that she bought, The Complete Idiot's Guide to Writing a Novel, by Tom Monteleone, she noticed that this author had written many books. Some of these were The Blood of the Lamb, in 1993, the sequel The Reckoning, in 2000 and The Eyes of the Virgin, in 2002. Then she realized the reason why she was advised to get this book. God knew his name was going to be mentioned, and this was a good example of how God honors those that honor Him.

"If anyone serves Me, let him follow Me; and where I am, there My servant will be also If anybody serves Me, him My Father will honor."
John 12:26

A contract is a legal document where both sides benefit; this is an earthly agreement. A covenant with God is a spiritual love agreement. He has established a relationship with us. We must walk with Him, knowing our obligations and responsibilities toward this friendship, without expecting compensation. Because we are not equal, expecting a reward for serving God is an unsuitable activity. When He bestows blessings on us, we must react with humility and appreciation. Consummating a covenant with us is pure grace on His part.

In Noah's time, God decided to destroy man and everything of flesh on earth. He was sorry He made us.

But Noah found grace in the eyes of the Lord. But I will establish My covenant with you; thus Noah did; according to all that God commanded him , so he did. Gen. 6:8, 18, 22

"I will never again curse the ground for man's sake although the imagination of man's heart is evil from his youth." Gen. 8:21

"I set My rainbow in the cloud, and it shall be for the sign of the covenant between Me and the earth." Gen. 9:13

GOD 'S COVENANT WITH CREATION.

* * *

When God reaffirmed a covenant with Abraham that the land will belong to his offspring forever, Abraham responded by building an altar to the Lord. Moses made a covenant with God to transform a collection of former slaves into a nation. The slaves had a difficult time keeping their side of the bargain to honor God. They kept slipping into deception, time and time again. Sin is the result of the need to keep covenant with God, which means if we want God to do His part (grant our petition prayers) than we must persevere with our intention of honoring Him. He will do what is best for our own interest or what is suitable for the plan He has for us.

THE CALVARY COVENANT

And the Word became flesh and dwelt among us, and we beheld His glory, the glory as of the only begotten of the Father, full of grace and truth. John 1:14

GOD SAID, "I WANT TO DWELL AMONG THEM."

AND THE WORD BECAME FLESH; JESUS CHRIST.

The covenant that Jesus made for our sins was on an even scale, because He is God. God's purpose is to have His creation reunited with Him. His concern for our salvation shows His nature, of a caring Father that wants us to follow the right path, but His divine profound humility cannot force us.

"For this is My blood of the new covenant which is shed for many for the remission of sins." Matt. 26:28

The greatest covenant made through Jesus is the action demonstrating the immeasurable integrity of God's love. This concept is quite difficult for some of us to grasp and envision. The reason for this statement is that we do not seem to realize the entitlement and the privilege of this valuable and precious manifestation that God did through His Son. By accepting Jesus' contribution and covenant we are being allowed to be clean of sin, therefore, creating a temple for the Lord to reside and live with us, making us His children. God is expecting our participation and declaration of faith in His Son, giving us the advantage of walking in confidence, trust, reliance, assurance, and conviction (faith). Attaining all these attributes and qualities is salvation here on earth and having the opportunity of salvation when we die (eternal life). On the subject of God's power and the sovereignty of God, the apostle Paul said,

"To whom pertain the adoption, the glory, the covenants, the giving of the law, the service of *God, and His promises."*
Rom. 9:4

JESUS' ACTION OF THE NEW COVENANT RESTED

DIRECTLY ON THE SACRIFICIAL ACT OF HIMSELF.

He is the Mediator of the new covenant. That those who are called may receive the promise of eternal inheritance. Heb. 9:15

Jesus' death and resurrection brought us the divine establishment of God's kingdom. He is the One that made it possible for us to have a relationship with the Father. He is the Mediator that brought us the three Spirits to live with us, the Son, The Father and the Holy Spirit all three in One God. This is possible because there is no space between spirits. These Spirits are like a divine essence that is alive with universal intelligence. It does not mean God is an essence, but He is the closest comparison to a Person not taking space. Some people perceive God as a metaphysical being, energy or a light. However, a profound mystical experience with God brings us to the reality and the profound awakening that dominates our entire thinking, coming to the realization of God's reality that needs no explanation. This mystery is not to be figured out through humanistic psychology, but rather to be enjoyed. We are tremendously fortunate to have the advantage of His love.

Our Christian journey and faith declares that God still desires and initiates covenant relationship with us, except it is more covenant community. Because of our baptism we have joined as a member in the body of Christ. Joining together is absolutely essential for the support that is required for a strong community. We need the willingness to express and encourage genuine care for the body of Christ.

Then indeed, even the first covenant had ordinances of divine service and the earthly sanctuary. Heb. 9:1

* * *

Anton became a believer in the covenant community. One night she was saying her prayers and asking for assistance and guidance for the family and what was required at the time. These were the usual prayers of a mother, **"Please God, help our children. Bless my daughter in law with a child. Help our son find a job. Keep us healthy, secure our jobs, and help us do and accept your will. Please God have mercy on us."** Suddenly she heard the Holy Spirit's vibrations, which surprised her, because the Spirit is not comfortable offering information on God‘s expectations of any specific problem. This is the reason why she makes a point of writing the message when He does give information without her asking, because it means it is an important issue. He is extremely respectful of people's free will.

The Holy Spirit's vibrations said, **"God wants you to make a sacrifice."** That immediately frightened Anton. She thought, **"Oh, my God, a sacrifice usually means something that is going to hurt."** The first thing that came to her mind was Abraham when he was asked to sacrifice Isaac to the Lord. Fortunately, it was nothing that her imagination was conjuring up. The sacrifice was for her to take a donation to her church. She was glad and relieved to find out the donation was the sacrifice. Anton is not a church person, so the request caught her by surprise. But, she does have a preference for one church although she figures God is everywhere.

A good number of Charismatic Christians do not belong to affiliated organizations because they feel affiliating with a local church can sometimes be disappointing. Most established religions have their own values, expressing their own beliefs and their own interpretations of God's laws. The members are expected to believe accordingly. This is the reason numerous people have chosen Spirituality and they just believe in God which is less dogmatic, because Spirituality only deals with the soul and spirit. Spirituality, offers a more personal relationship with the divine power. People can be solitary believers obligated to no one but themselves and God.

However, we must realize that as Christians we are obligated to the mystical body of Jesus Christ, even if we disagree about the interpretation of the Bible's theology. The church is not just a building, but a place to host God's people; the church is human.

Now, therefore, you are no longer strangers and foreigners,
but fellow citizens with the saints and members of the household of God.
Eph. 2:19

When Jesus first drew His followers, He did not turn them in upon themselves. Immediately He sent them to treat massive hurts of spirits and body that festered in the world around them. When He spoke of the community that would abide eternally in God's presence, it clearly would be the community of those who fed the hungry, welcomed the strangers, clothed the naked, cared for the sick, and visited the prisoner.

Stephen V. Doughty

When Anton took the love offering to the church, she noticed that when the offerings were laid at the alter, the layman said, **"I want for all of us to pray for the sacrifices you all have offered."** It caught her by surprise, because she did not remember this expression of referring to the donations as sacrifices. All she knew for sure was that this was the confirmation of what the vibrations of the Holy Spirit had suggested for her to do.

Today tithing, love offerings and money donations are pleasing to God and are forms of sacrifice, because life is difficult for many Christians. The rich man who gives up his riches is not as pleasing to the Father as is the widow who gave her last two cents to the Lord.

"Assuredly, I say to you that this poor widow has put in more than all those who have given to the treasury." Mark 12:43

The new covenant through Jesus' blood, is not exclusive to our benefit here on earth. God's promise was to be with us, but Jesus suggested a new level of servitude and obedience. This suggestion of being obedient children might touch God's heart, having the possibility of a blessing come upon us and our prayers answered. Everything is by grace, but He does honor the faithful. If He does not answer in the affirmative immediately, we still know He has our best interest at heart. We must be patient and understand that He sees the whole picture, while we can only see a couple of pieces of the puzzle at one time.

"Most assuredly, I say to you, I am the door of the sheep. If anyone enters by me, he will be saved, and will go in and out and find pasture." John 10:7, 9

With Him [Jesus] also comes a new people which the New Testament calls the *ekklesia* (church). Like the people of the Old Israel, they are called into being by God himself---to be His agent in this world until Christ' second coming.

James H. Cone

So I have looked for You in the sanctuary, To see Your power and Your glory. Because Your loving kindness is better than life, My lips shall praise You. Thus I will bless You while I live; I will lift up my hands in Your name. My soul shall be satisfied as with marrow and fatness, And my mouth shall praise You with joyful lips. Ps. 63:2-5

Prayer

The act of believing is important for prayers to be answered.

It is Christ who died, and furthermore is also risen, who is even at the right hand of God, who also make intercession for us. Rom. 8:34

Having God's glory is better than winning the lottery. Anton, human that she is, in the beginning of her relationship with the Holy Spirit tried to get the right lottery ticket numbers without success. It was not in God's plan. She realizes this now that she has a deeper relationship with Him. Our humanness cannot escape selfishness. When we live devoted to our senses, it is natural to seek enjoyment, pleasure and gratification. But, when God transforms us into illuminated beings (anointed) He will reveal a brilliance that awakens our consciousness and will deliver us from delusional dreams. We see the world objectively, resulting in maturity and humility. We come to the realization that there is a purpose for everything that happens in our life. God is in control and our guide. Worrying subsides, because we know God is now our Father and Friend, not just our Master. It is not too difficult to know what our friend is thinking and what is pleasant to Him. When we reach this higher level of consciousness, the guessing of life stops **"should I do this or that?"** We have broken the wall that separates us from doing God's will.

A short book by Raymond Finch, The Power of Prayer, relates good information about praying.

Millions pray: The most sensational new evidence strongly indicates that prayer can magically heal and prevent disease. But researchers all over the world are also finding that prayer may

help you become more successful, save your marriage or even help you lose weight.

Instinctive: There is no question that for many people prayer is an essential component of a happy and fulfilled life. We find in studies of primitive tribes that there seems to be an instinctive quality to pray, as if from the very core of our earthly selves we somehow feel compelled to launch our own private voyage into the unknown world of the spirit.

He also points out that people who pray often and meditate on the word of God seem to be more tranquil. These people do not blame God for transgressions or natural disasters. They do not believe God punishes humans or is vindictive. These faithful people give thanks and are appreciative of the prayers that are answered. Interesting enough, they also do not pray for material things. Instead, they seem to preserve spiritual love that adds meaning to their lives.

* * *

"Let not your heart be troubled; you believe in God, believe also in Me. Most assuredly, I say to you, he who believes in Me, the works that I do he will do also, and greater works than these he will do, because I go to My Father." John 14:1, 12

Dr. Larry Dossey a former chief of staff at Medical Dallas Hospital wrote a book entitled, Healing Words: The Power of Prayer and the Practice of Medicine.

Dr. Dossey mentions in his book, that more than 130 studies have taken place in how prayer can benefit patients with high blood pressure, heart attacks, wounds and anxiety. He is amazed how prayer works even when people are distant from the person they are praying for. He says, **"Nothing seems capable of stopping or blocking prayer."**

Dr. Dossey speculates that in a way prayer does not travel to God or to the person that is being prayed for, but it actually has what is called as no locality. He theorizes that the time-honored reason of explaining this phenomenon is that it works simultaneously everywhere. In his studies and experiments it has been discovered that prayer does not contain any kind of conventional form of energy. He says, **"If it did prayer would deteriorate as distance is increased."**

* * *

Paul the apostle wrote that we should pray for the growth of the church. Paul recognized that we need to be ministers of God's word. Apostles, prophets, evangelists, pastors, and teachers work hard, but one person cannot do all the work of Jesus' ministry. We must all be trained to be ministers for the growth and success of His body.

Prayer for Spiritual Wisdom

Do not cease to give thanks for you, making mention of you in my prayers: that the God of our Lord Jesus Christ, the Father of glory, may give to you the spirit of wisdom and revelation in the knowledge of Him. The eyes of your understanding being enlightened; that you may know what is the hope of His calling, what are the riches of the glory of His inheritance in saints, and what is the exceeding greatness of His power toward us who believe, according to the working of His mighty power. Eph. 1:16-19

It is necessary not to forget to say, **"Amen"** after a prayer. Amen is professing, declaring, and affirming our faith and putting a seal on the prayer. This seal will prevent tampering and will protect our words from the enemy. Saying amen, in a way, is like saying **"Thank You for hearing my prayers."** Amen also symbolizes our faith and trust in our Lord.

Two blind men followed Jesus, crying out loud and saying,

"Son of David, have mercy on us!" And Jesus said to them, "Do you believe that I am able to do this?" They said to Him, "Yes, Lord." Then He touched their eyes, saying, "According to your faith

let it be to you." And their eyes were opened. Matt. 9:27-30

Another important prayer that we must never neglect is to pray for our enemies and the enemies of the Nation. Pray that God will reveal Himself to them and turn their hearts to believers of the truth. Isaiah the prophet prophesies about the unbelievers.

He has blinded their eyes and hardened their hearts, lest they should see with their eyes, lest they should understand with their hearts and turn, so that "I should heal them." John 12:40

John the apostle said, **"God is light and in Him there is no darkness at all."** He also wrote,

For if our heart condemns us, God is greater than our heart, and knows all things. 1 John 3:20

There has to be an acquirement of fullness of God to be able not to be deceived by false prophets. **"The kingdom of God is at hand."** Through prayer and meditation the Holy Spirit abiding in us is able to do all things. When we have the richness of God, we find ourselves more frequently than occasionally, on speculative reasoning in which our perception is sufficient validity of His enlightenment. There is no need for division because our spirit will be joined with His; thus, making us aware of God being **"All sufficiency in all Things."** The Spirit abiding in us is the Eminent Creator of all things manifesting Himself through us. The manifestation of the reality of the Creator living in us depends on our ability to accept and recognize the truth. His sanctification and justification (alignment with God) will manifest in us when we have the recognition and the trust of His divine presence, which is His Eminent Holiness. His divine life is always perfect, strong and vigorous in us, and through prayer it will flow to our problems and to other human beings. We will experience physical recognition and acceptance of ourselves and others.

"If anyone loves Me, he will keep My word; and My Father will

love him, and We will come to him and make Our home with him."
John 14:23

In prayer we open ourselves to the chance that God will do something with us that we had not intended.

Emilie Griffin

Affirmative prayer will turn our thoughts and faith to the Almighty, bringing the necessities of our life to our existence. Prayer takes us beyond our human selves. We feel that something exists beyond our human senses that cannot be understood. Even the worst of prayers makes us reach further than ourselves. It is essential to visualize the results of our prayer and to thank God in anticipation.

Some people feel they our bothering God when they ask for help with small problems. In fact, we are actually acknowledging God's presence and it is a form of worship. God's wisdom, power and understanding in our lives are an expression of His love. This is a source of deep consolation, although we do not understand the whole concept. God infinitely understands the plan that He has for His children.

The concept of being made in God's image has intrigued and challenged theologians in every generation. Perhaps, it is our spirit, since God is all Spirit. The exact form does not matter. What matters is that God has given us a share in His own image. Through Jesus Christ He revealed his image to mankind, so we might once more come to know him. And because we are made in God's image is precisely the reason that prayer is so important. God's word has power; therefore, our word has power. The word can become Spirit and life like Jesus. When God decided to dwell among us, He must have said the word, and it reached culmination in the sending of His Son.

And the word became flesh and dwelt among us, and we beheld His glory, the glory as the only begotten of the Father, full of grace and truth. John 1:14

Our word does not have the same power as God, but it does indeed have some power. Uttering the word can certainly materialize in the physical realm, depending on how the spiritual realm perceives and captures it. If it is God's will, it will penetrate into creative activity.

Anton found this concept when she asked the Holy Spirit, **"How does prayer work?"**The vibrations of the Spirit answered, **"Your word has power."** She was getting a big head, until she looked it up in the Bible. It stated that indeed everybody's word has power, since we are made in God's image. God spoke the word first and Jesus became the word in flesh.

"You understand my thought afar off. And are acquainted with all my ways. For there is no word on my tongue, But behold, O Lord, You know it altogether." Ps. 139:2-4

We can bring into visible form that which does not exist. In fact, there is no other way to bring into existence the visible things we desire, if not through the spoken word. The material realm and the spiritual are intangible in the atmosphere. Even though the spiritual realm is invisible the two realms are blended into one, making it impossible to distinguish where one begins and another ends.

Taking our thoughts out of the visible world, focusing and centering our prayers into the spiritual formless substance with faith will give us a better opportunity for our prayers to come to pass.

* * *

H. Emilie Cady wrote a book titled, <u>HOW I USED TRUTH</u>. She found that through affirmative prayer she attained answers to her prayers. Through faith she was able to reach beyond her own existence. She shares her message with conviction on how to reach the Lord and find answers to our problems.

"Almost every one of the simply written articles in <u>How I Used Truth</u> was born out of the travail of my soul after I had

been weeks, months, sometimes years, trying by affirmations, by claiming the promises of Jesus, and by otherwise faithfully using all knowledge of Truth that I then possessed to secure deliverance for myself or others from some distressing bondage that thus far had defied all human help."

She asks no one to believe what is written in her book simply because it is presented as truth. **"Prove all things,"** she says. She feels it would not be impossible to prove every statement in her book because every statement has been proved before it was written. Cady states that **"No person can solve another's problem for him."**

Each person must work out his own problems and salvation. She feels that some effectual rules and ideas that are suggested in her writing will obtain results, but it will depend on how faithfully and persistently the person uses the advice given in the book.

The author is grateful for the numerous words of appreciation that have come to her from time to time. The feedback is encouraging she says, **"To one who is trying to solve her own life's problems,"** just as we all are trying to solve ours by the teaching of the Almighty.

* * *

Prayer takes us beyond our human selves. We can feel that something exists beyond our senses and cannot be understood. We all know that we do not use the full capacity of our brain; it is said that we only use one fraction. Since we are all in that predicament, we should be open to introductions of other people's beliefs and their relationship to the Lord. There is no structure or organization that any one person can say is the correct way to accomplish an answer from the Lord. We are inadequate to comprehend the foundational elements in how God works in our lives. There are many questions that remain unclear. We should continually seek to communicate with Him, opening ourselves to a deep personal relationship. Prayer is to surrender ourselves to the Lord. The main quality of prayer is accepting the will of God with a pure open heart.

Who has not lifted up his soul to an idol, nor sworn deceitfully. He shall receive blessings from the Lord, and righteousness from the God of his salvation. Ps. 24:4-5

"God is Spirit and those who worship Him must worship in spirit and truth." John 4:24

Even the worst of prayers makes us reach beyond ourselves. This was illustrated to the writer. A woman, Miss S---, had been divorced for eight years. She was talking to a friend and said, **"I think I would like to get married again if I could find the right man."** The friend responded, **"Let's pray to God."** Jokingly, she said, "What qualifications do you want in him?" Miss S--- laughingly said, **"I want him to be handsome, crazy about me, kind of tall, and to have a little money."** By saying with a little money she did not want to sound too demanding. She was not confident, and was unaware that she was, **"Speaking the word"** out into the great universe of substance for something she much desired. Within six months Miss S--- was married to the man of her dreams. It is amazing, but we just never know when God's providence will come upon us. The word spoken by Miss S--- in the conversation had shaped and brought forth toward the physical realm, from the spiritual realm, the thing she desired. The words she had uttered permeated to the unknown, creating an action invisible to the physical realm. The word continued shaping the action, eventually bringing the shape of the action forth into the visible world as a solid manifestation of exactly what Miss S--- had spoken. It is very important to have God in our minds at all times, for we do not know when He is in agreement and will prepare the ground for our desires. God is busy behind the scenes pulling everything else together so those prayers are answered in just the right way. That is if the prayer is with the right motives and a thankful heart, He will take care of the rest. When we have the knowingness of God, the more certain we are of His will. We will know what is important to Him.

If we honor the Lord, He will reciprocate as He did with Moses. When the children of Israel complained, then He gave them bread (manna from heaven).

"For you have brought us into the wilderness to kill this whole assembly with hunger." Then The Lord said to Moses, "Behold I will rain bread from heaven for you." Ex. 16:3-4

If God is not in agreement with our petition prayer it will not happen no matter how hard we pray. He has another plan for the situation of our life. Our intellectual questioning of a prayer will only lead us to a crisis of faith. We need to take in consideration that God analyzes the request totally, resulting in what is appropriate for the person and the body of the believers. He is in charge of the equilibrium of the body for the good of mankind. Having faith means we trust the Lord without feeling discouraged about His understanding of our prayers. Surrendering to His will is difficult at times. When Jesus asked the Father,

"Father if it is Your will, take this cup away from Me; nevertheless not My will, but Yours, be done." Luke 22:42

The request of taking the cup away from Jesus was not in line with the word of the Father. Jesus had to be crucified in order to save believers. This was the will of the Father. Faith can remove mountains, but that still has to be in line with God's will.

"For assuredly, I say to you, whoever says to this mountain, 'Be removed and cast into the sea,' and does not doubt in his heart, but believers that those things he says will be done." Mark 11:23

Only when we are able to "let go" of everything within us, all desire to see, to know, to taste and experience the presence of God, do we truly become able to experience that presence with the overwhelming conviction and reality that revolutionizes our entire inner life.

Thomas Merton

Worship

The true worship of God is to surrender to His will and reach beyond ourselves, realizing something more exists than our physical senses.

"God is Spirit and those who worship Him must worship in Spirit and truth." John 4:24

Even though both Pam and Anton love the Lord, it was a tremendous challenge to write this book. Because they came from such different backgrounds, there were times when Pam would have a difficult time trying to figure out what Anton was trying to convey. And then there were times when they completely disagreed on the subject. Pam refused to type what she did not believe to be true, because she was committed to her religious beliefs. The Holy Spirit filled them with the ability, intelligence and knowledge in order to be able to understand one another. Their love for the Lord helped them rise above any worldly concerns they had and any differences of opinion about one another's beliefs. Ultimately, they would get to the final analysis with God's grace.

For example, Anton believes Christians have a responsibility to leave a legacy behind after their death. Our mission here is to make a difference in this world that God loves so much, to see if we can leave **"a little grain"** to make the world a better place. Thus, we will make Christ's body stronger. This affiliation has to be equipped with hope, unity of faith and glory.

Christ also loved the church and gave Himself for her, that He might sanctify and cleanse her with the washing of water by the word. Eph. 5:25-26

On the other hand, Pam believes, **"Mankind is here only to worship God."** This woman knows the Bible well, even though she does not consider herself an expert. This idea is in opposition to Anton's beliefs, even though she knows in her heart just how important it is to worship God. But, is God's only intention for humans just to worship Him? She would argue with Pam about this philosophical difference. Their discussions would get quite vocal. It was difficult to understand each others mentality, especially since both women came from such different life experiences. Anton's perception is that God knows man is totally imperfect after the fall of Adam and Eve. He merely wants us to do the best that we can in worshiping and serving Him. To make these commitments an easier task for humankind, God sent his precious Son Jesus. Through His Son, He sent the world a new message; His unconditional love, forgiveness and sacrifice and the opportunity of being saved under God's grace. In return we should be humble, joyfully obedient and radiating the power of His love.

Holy Jesus, make me acknowledge Thee to be my Lord and Master, and myself a servant and disciple of Thy holy discipline and institution.

Jeremy Taylor

After much praying, discussion and arguments Anton decided to ask the Holy Spirit who was correct in their beliefs---Pam or her---and there was no response from the Spirit. This is how people know when God is communicating with them. He will never advise a person to create adversity between friends or family members. If a person thinks that they hear a voice telling them to do harm or think negatively with impure thoughts against another person, then we know that is not from God or any part of the Holy Trinity.

Anton believes Jesus came into this world to make a difference and to show us how to love one another. He did this by making the ultimate sacrifice. Therefore, **"Actions speak louder than words."** Allowing the crucifixion to take place proves that Jesus loved us so much that He sacrificed his body in order to save us from an eternity in hell. He came and left us a tremendous legacy that completely changed the world. Why then, would we be any different? We are certainly not being asked to suffer in the exact manner. But God does expect us to go out of our way to help others. This is not easy since we all are very self-absorbed and lead very busy and complicated lives. God has commissioned us to pass on our faith, help unbelievers and make a little difference in this world just like Jesus, who came to teach us the word of God and ultimate love. He left us such a remarkable example, so how can anybody read His life story and not try to emulate His actions? It is important to leave a legacy, whether it is having children or helping others in their lives. The main thing is to make sure we bear fruit. Paul the disciple worked hard for the Lord. He knew we are justified by faith, but we will stand before Christ where our works will be judged, not our sins, for they were judged on the cross in the body of Jesus. James the disciple thought dead faith produces dead works.

But someone will say, "You have faith, and I have works." Show me your faith without your works, and I will show you my faith by my works. James 2:18

These ladies knew a man, and we will call him John out of respect. He was in his 50's, married twice, unsuccessfully, with no children, and dramatically depressed. It seemed like he did not know what life was all about. He was a good man, but he resented taking care of his elderly mother. He condemned those who did not do the right things, which frustrated him more. He did not want to hear anybody with a positive attitude telling him God loved him. He would answer, **"So why is life so depressing?"**

To the surprise of these ladies, John caught a virus and died within a few days before his mother who was eighty five years old. God probably thought that He had given this man plenty of time to redeem himself and know what life was all about. God must have decided to end his misery, because how does a healthy man suddenly get a strange virus and die? There was an unsuccessful investigation to discover where he might have contracted the virus.

This is more proof to Anton that we have a mission in this life to accomplish. God wants us to be His light, to try to guide and rescue as many souls as possible out of the dark. We are honoring mankind and God with this effort. One of our commissions of baptism is to be a minister of His word. Jesus said,

"For I come down from heaven, not to do My will, but the will of Him who sends Me." John 6:38

Anton is not very knowledgeable about the Bible, but she can make a good argument. Pam told Anton to ask the Holy Spirit again, if we are to leave a legacy or just worship God? By now both had agreed to agree to disagree. The two women realized that they both still had the right for some degree of autonomy in their firm beliefs in God's word and how it affected their hearts and spirits. Even though they had been arguing this theological point, they both knew there was a time to settle the argument and when to leave it alone. Both ladies concluded that the first time they had asked the question about the matter, they were not ready to hear the answer. They were too stubborn in their beliefs and in their theological concepts. But, after much discussion they understood that as long as they loved and respected one another, they had the right and freedom to believe in their beliefs. The Holy Spirit's vibrations answered and got to the point, **"Pam is right. All you have to do is worship the Lord."**

The definition of the word "worship" in the Webster's Dictionary Thesaurus & Atlas is,

Worship 1-Adoration, homage, etc., given to a deity. 2-The rituals, prayers, etc. expressing such adoration or homage. 3-Excessive or ardent admiration or love. 4-The object of such love or admiration. 5-*Chiefly Brit.* A title of honor in addressing certain persons of station. To pay an act of worship; venerate. To have intense or exaggerated admiration or love for. To perform acts or have sentiments of worship.

IF WE CONSTANTLY THINK AND PRAISE GOD,

IT WILL BRING US INTO FELLOWSHIP WITH HIM.

To love the Lord in a worshiping manner is to remove our senses and be dominated by His will. Biblical worshiping involves the total person, so all our senses are called into action. Our senses are a fantasy of this world. They belong to the old us before our baptism. When we become a new creature in Christ, we need to dispose of all our senses and live in His presence. It is wonderful when we see the light of this important theological concept of worshiping God and understanding all we need is His grace. A mature Christian life is Spirit centered and constitutes living in Christ. So it is actually the Lord who is working through us; we are His vessels (recipients who embody quality.) Jesus' own self-image was embodied with God's Spirit.

"I have been crucified with Christ; it is no longer I who live, but Christ lives in me; and the life which I now live in the flesh I live by faith in the Son of God, who loved me and gave Himself for me." Gal. 2:20

It is a noble goal to try to leave a Christian legacy and a tremendous beautiful vision of human capacity to strive to be like Jesus, however, God knows our weaknesses as humans and it would be impossible. This is precisely the reason He equipped us with the Holy Spirit. It is difficult to do actions of good works out of a sense of human duty. Charity by design becomes spontaneous if we accept the virtues that come from the indwelling of the Holy Spirit. Our faithfulness toward God and our appropriate behavior should be the result of a true association that we have with God, thus, feeling a sense of purpose and love. Concerning mankind, we need grace that comes directly from the results of our faith and our love for the Creator.

WE NEED GOD'S GRACE IN ORDER TO

EXPERIENCE MERCY, LOVE, COMPASION AND PATIENCE.

Therefore it is of faith that it might be according to grace, so

that the promise might be sure to all the seed, not only to those who are of the law, but also to those who are of the faith of Abraham.
Rom. 4:16

God's grace is not divided into bits and pieces... but grace takes us up completely into God's favor for the sake of Christ, our intercessor and mediator, so that the gifts [of the Spirit] may begin their work.

Martin Luther

God's grace works through us if we are faithful to His word. However, a constant warfare exists here on earth between evil and good. There is a fantasy that impedes the real vision God has for Christians. This fantasy believes Christians are immune to evil. This is not true we need to be vigilant and constantly fight with ourselves to stay in the word. We must realize the effort needed to achieve complete abandonment of ourselves and let the Lord work through us. Achieving this goal will keep us in touch with the interior of our spirit, perceiving the presence of the Lord that escapes human reality and waking up the desire to share the love and joy of God.

Perceiving: This chapter points us back to meditation. Studying the word of the Lord with concentration and repetition will automatically transcend us into contemplation, which is being in the presence of the Lord. Meditating in His word faithfully and frequently will renew our mind, soul and spirit. This process of feeling God's presence is different in each individual, according to the person's ability to perceive objectively His existence. As we experience the renewal of our being, God penetrates and envelops us with His presence.

Through our baptism we receive the Holy Spirit, enabling us with the understanding of God's word and being able to accomplish a personal encounter with Jesus and God. The Holy Spirit also has the capability of conducting a dialogue with The Lord. We are the only beings in creation that have the ability to overcome limitations of our senses and become One with the Creator. It is not us that exist anymore, but the Lord abiding in us. By worshiping God, we will experience living in the center of our being, which is our spirit and His. It is where the Holy Spirit resides; therefore, all the good deeds and works of faith are done by God through us.

"Thus also faith by itself, if it does not have works, is dead." James 2:17

Paul wrote about living faith given by God.

"For by grace you have been saved through faith, and that not of yourselves; it is a gift of God, not of works, lest anybody should boast." Eph. 2:8-9

As we study and meditate on God's word we come to understand the value and the mechanics of the energy forces involved for a transformed life; union with God. We acquire the information necessary for this transition. This will help us to enter our new life with the confidence and assurance of having the presence of God within.

* * *

When we hear that Mother Teresa suffered tremendously because she did not feel God's presence, it surprises us to think that even this saintly lady did not know she had arrived at the goal of becoming one with God. It was almost as if God had put up a veil, and she could not see the reality. There is something very significant to learn from Teresa's secret letters to her superiors and confessors, especially about her agony from not sensing the presence of God for almost a half century. The letters were made public a decade after her death. She wanted them to be destroyed, but eventually she decided it could help people see her mission as a blind faith call. She probably decided the letters would help Christians in the world that do not feel the presence of God and have doubts of God's existence. Nobody could ever imagine that a world-famous saint like her did not have an intimate relationship with the Lord and did not feel His presence. One can only admire the extraordinary and ardent faith of this woman. Teresa lived in torment all those years, because she considered the absence of God in her life as a shameful secret. The phenomenon here is that people could perceive the presence of the Lord in her and see the love and serenity that could only come from God. She had a divine gift that enabled her to do great work for the Lord.

"Seeing they may see and not perceive, And hearing they may hear and not understand." Mark 4:12

Christians that experience the presence of God can surely understand her torment and agony. Because, when we perceive the presence of God, there is nothing to compare it with in the world. He becomes our passion, the reason for our existence like the air we breathe. He is the reason for our smiles and the love in our being. It gives us enthusiasm and energy for life. One can only imagine how desolate Mother Teresa must have felt to experience the abandonment of God. It must be terribly disappointing to at one time feel His presence and for it to suddenly disappear. She referred to her life as **"my darkness"** and Jesus as **"the Absent One."** Her loneliness never stopped her from working in the Missionary of the Pure Heart home for the dying in Calcutta.

Mother Teresa gave her life to the Lord. He used her as his vessel to help the poor, and in her death she is still helping Christians in their spiritual growth. She assists us with the knowledge that even a saint like her can fall into a psychological trap of thinking God is not with her. She is the example of not being aware that our spiritual growth eventually comes to a termination and when it is finished we become One with Him. We reach the highest point a human can attain in the evolution of feeling God's presence. It is a process and, of course, we are going to feel His presence when we are being transformed. A transformation is taking place with different manifestations, emotions, sensations, and supernatural feelings of another entity closing into our spirit with tremendous love. God has arrived to our neurological center, transforming us into the greatness of Jesus. It is difficult for some to feel the presence of an entity that has become One with us. Jesus said,

"I and the Father are One." John 10:30

"Now I am no longer in the world, but these are in the world, and I come to You Holy Father, keep through your name those whom You have given Me, that they may be One as We are." John 17:11

WHEN WE GIVE UP OUR RESISTANCE OF THE FLESH TO THE TRANSFORMATION OF BECOMING ONE AND SURRENDERING OUR WILL, WE WILL BE REFLECTING THE PRESENCE OF THE LORD.

There is an interesting article in TIME magazine, "The Secret Life of Mother Teresa" by David Van Biema, September 3, 2007. It tells us about Mother Teresa hearing form the Lord, but it also indicates her state of peacefulness. She was ordered to relax by her superiors. This is how it reads,

On Sep. 10, 1946, after 17 years as a teacher in Calcutta with the Loreto Sisters (an uncloistered, education-oriented community based in Ireland), Mother Teresa, 36, took the 400-mile (645-km) train trip to Darjeeling. She had been working herself sick, and her superiors ordered her to relax during her annual retreat in the Himalayan foothills. On the ride out, she reported, Christ spoke to her. He called her to abandon teaching and work instead in "the slums" of the city, dealing directly with "the poorest of the poor"---the sick, the dying, beggars and street children. "Come, come, carry Me into the holes of the poor," He told her. "Come be My light." The goal was to be both material and evangelistic-- as Kolodiejchuk puts it, "to help them live their lives with dignity [and so] encounter God's infinite love, and having come to know Him, to love and serve Him in return."

After the Vatican gave permission for her to embark on her second calling, she felt Jesus had taken Himself away from her. Of course, there have been various speculations and theories of why Teresa did not feel the presence of the Lord. Here are a few; purification for a strong personality or grace enhancing the efficacy of her calling. (The worst speculation that most Christians refuse to believe, is that the abandonment was the result of high achievement which certain personalities punished themselves and making her the author of her own misery.)

A letter to Jesus from Mother Teresa at the suggestion of her confessor is sad to read. In the same article in TIME magazine, this is a part of the letter.

Lord, my God, who am I that You should forsake me? The child of your love--and now become as the most hated one--the one--You have thrown away as unwanted--unloved. I call, I cling, I want--and there is no One to answer--no One on Whom I can cling--on, No One.--Alone...Where is my faith--even deep down right in there is nothing, but emptiness & darkness--My God--how painful is this unknown pain--I have no faith--I dare not utter the words & thoughts that crowd in my heart.

* * *

We need to understand the makeup of this saintly woman and her strong, complex character, to be able to comprehend how she arrived to such a tormented and desolate state. First of all, she was a very active person. She did things with love, passion, conviction, perseverance, eagerness, and enthusiasm. She was an achiever with extraordinary faith, willing to be an ardent servant of the Lord. To have all these qualities takes an enormous amount of energy and concentration. A person of her caliber had to be thinking constantly of what was done yesterday, what is going to be accomplished today, and what the plan is for tomorrow. Perhaps, it was difficult for this modern saint to quiet her preoccupied mind to be able to hear the Lord's whispers. Meditating on God's word takes tremendous dedication of the mind, blanking out any worries of our problems, intentions or resolutions that we might be thinking of for this complicated life. She was an extreme example of a person who was always thinking about how to ease the pain of others. We saw numerous pictures of her praying, but was she objectively thinking in the prayer, engulfing herself in the grace of God, appreciating the gift that it is to accomplish being in His presence. We will never know, but we can learn from this saintly, faithful woman and all the theories that are out there about the reasons for her torment.

* * *

Through baptism we receive the Holy Spirit; however, to become One with Him is only through grace. It is a gift. When we become One with Him, we will probably not feel His presence. This is the reason we need to concentrate, to quiet our mind in order to be able to penetrate into our subconscious where we can decode the vibrations of the Holy Spirit. Then, we will actually receive private revelations that are only designed for our spirit and soul, for the purpose God has for our lives. Paul the disciple wrote,

The God of our Lord Jesus Christ, the father of glory, may give you the spirit of wisdom and revelation in the knowledge of Him The eyes of your understanding being enlightened; that you may know what is the hope of His calling , what are the riches of the glory of His inheritance in His saints. Eph. 1:17-18

Worship, in all its grades and kinds, is the response of creatures to the Eternal: nor need we limit this definition to the human sphere. There is a sense in which we may think of the whole life of the Universe, seen and unseen, conscious and unconscious, as an act of worship, glorifying its Origin, Sustainer, and End.

Evelyn Underhill

Chapter 7

THE CHURCH

The church (the body of Christ) is a community that has received the Holy Spirit and has the responsibility as Ministers toward service for the future of the church.

The manifestation of the Spirit is given to each one for the profit of all.
1 Cor. 12:7

It is a mystery why some Christians suffer more then others. People have different theories, but the truth is we actually do not know how the body of Christ functions, which deals with the past, present and future. We are oblivious of the struggles and conflicts Christ has to wage for the protection of the body. The body is composed and united by Christians and Children of God in grace through faith. Believers compose a community; the body of Christ. Christ rules and sustains the body to bring balance for our salvation. He is the head of the body; the Godhead. God is always preserving unity in His mystical way by fusing us with the meaning of life through mercy, goodness, acceptance, forgiveness and hope. One only needs to stay vigilant in the fight against evil that oppresses and dehumanizes the body of Christ. We can protect ourselves with God's strength, His unconditional love and forgiveness of our sins. There are no sociopsychological answers to the understanding of the fundamental uniqueness of how God protects us and His concern for the mystical body. Our theological knowledge does not understand the cosmic vision that God has for the salvation of the human race. As mentioned before, only when we accidentally confront our own mystery (communion with God) can we comprehend our **"being here"** and understand our existence, our evolvement, and the plan He has for us. The mystery of the church was revealed to Paul and other apostles by the Holy Spirit.

From whom the whole body, joined and knit together by what every joint supplies, according to the effective working by which every part does its share, causes growth of the body for the edifying of itself in love. Eph. 4:16

Paul knew the importance of bringing balance to the body of Christ through suffering. God allows believers to experience tribulations and pain for the accomplishment of His purpose in our lives. God wants all His children to inherit salvation. This is precisely the reason that God sent His only begotten Son to die on the cross. Christians are adopted in the blood line through Christ, giving us the opportunity of salvation through His suffering. Paul urges every believer to be accepting and conform to the perfect will of God.

Living Sacrifices to God

"I beseech you therefore, brethren, by the mercies of God, that you present your bodies a living sacrifice, holy, acceptable to God, which is your reasonable service. And do not be conformed to this world, but be transformed by the renewing of your mind, that you may prove what is that good and acceptable and perfect will of God." Rom. 12:1

Christians are predestined to contribute suffering or work as Ministers of His word for the edification and glorification of the body of Christ. Some Christians, like Paul, seemed to be called to do both. Jesus will share His grace and glory with these Christians who do the will of God. Paul said,

"For whom He foreknew, He predestined to be conformed to the image of His Son, that He might be the firstborn among many brethren. Moreover whom He predestine, these He also called; whom He called, these He

also justified; and whom He justified, these He also glorified." Rom. 8:29-30

"For we have many members in one body, but all the members do not have the same function." Rom. 12:4

The disciple Paul understood the power of Christ rested on him through his infirmities and how he sustained Christians in the body of Christ, for those that were called to be sanctified in Christ. Paul realize that he would rather be sick, persecuted and in distress, than not to have God's strength to preach His word.

For none of us lives to himself, and no one dies to himself. Rom. 14:7

Paul's mind was enlightened to understand the whole equation and evolution of the body of Christ. He was predestined to be conformed to the image of Christ.

We then who are strong ought to bear with scruples of the weak, and not please ourselves. Let each of us please his neighbor for his good, leading to edification. Rom. 15:1-2

THE INNOCENT PAYING FOR THE GUILTY.

No, much rather, those members of the body which seem to be weaker are necessary. And those members of the body which we think to be less honorable, on these we bestow greater honor; and our unpresentable parts have greater modesty, but our presentable parts have no need. But God composed the body, having given greater honor to that part which lacks it, that there should be no schism in the body, but that member should have the same care for one another. 1 Cor. 12:22-25

This part of the Bible brings light to the understanding of doing penance for other souls and offering our pain to the Lord. The Christians that suffer the most in this world do extra glorifying to the body in which we all coexist. It all depends where the most support of the body of Christ is needed. Jesus places individuals where their destiny is to be martyrs, either for the family or just other souls in the body. Actually, Christians who have a good life and good health are being subsidized and are profiting from others. We should precondition ourselves to be grateful for our good fate and our good fortune to those other individuals who were predestined to have greater difficulties and hardship in this world. Paul knew this well and said,

"Be kindly affectionate to one another with brotherly love, in honor giving preference to one another." Rom. 12:10

But now indeed there are many members, yet one body. And the eye cannot say to the hand, "I have no need of you;" nor again the head to the feet, "I have no need of you." 1 Cor. 12:20-21

We must not think of ourselves independently. We are all members of the body, and we belong to each other. Therefore, we should all be honored. Each of us has a duty to God to pursue and perform. Each member has been given different abilities, concerns, gifts and insights. God commands us not to criticize each other for our interest in the different ways that we serve God. Some Christians have a quality of mystery and ambiguity that makes them difficult to understand. However, they are still contributing to the glory of the body. Paul tells us we are all ambassadors of Christ and recommends that we be considerate and sympathetic.

"For I say, through the grace given to me, to everyone who is among you, not to think of himself more highly than he ought to think, but to think soberly, as God has dealt to each one a measure of faith." Rom. 12:3

Understanding the other side of the equation is mysteriously wonderful, because Jesus has taken our tribulations, transgressions and infirmities into purification for the glory and grace of the edifying of the body of believers. Christians who have suffered will get their reward sooner or later. Their pain has been purified into glory. We hear of people who have terrible and hurtful upbringings who, later in life, find the Lord. They start to walk in faith, and they discover that there is nothing more wonderful and fantastic than having a personal intimate relationship with the Lord. Another act that turns into glory is when we are gracious, charitable, caring, compassionate and helpful to others. Various individuals may not receive their reward in this life, but must wait until they arrive in heaven. Paul knew this to be so for him, but he did not care and remained adamant and passionate about his mission on earth,

But I want you to know, brethren that the things which happen to me have actually turned out for the furtherance of the gospel, so that it has become evident to the whole palace guard, and to all the rest, that my chains are in Christ. What then? Only that in every way, whether in pretence or in truth, Christ is preached; and in this I rejoice, yes, and will rejoice. Phil. 1:12-13, 18

* * *

Reliance: Some Preachers preach the word of faith. They have the knowledge of what the body of Christ contains. God reveals to them the magnificent glory and grace that has been accomplished through Jesus Christ and His followers to form His body; a Christian organization which has accumulated a great amount of goods for the growth and protection of its members. To tap into these riches we must profess the word of faith in the Father, Son and Holy Spirit. Jesus suffered for our sins. Jesus told us we would suffer transgressions, because He knew the enemy reigns in the world. But God outsmarted him and used his offenses and wrong doings to help us pay our dues to maintain the body strong. God sent His Son as an example of how the spiritual realm works, how pain and suffering purifies wrongs. However, if we are going to suffer, then we might as well enjoy the glory and grace of what the body has to offer though faith. Our inheritance also includes spiritual riches such as forgiveness, righteousness, holiness, eternal life and bliss with Jesus. The Messianic body of the Lord has peace, truth, happiness, kindness, beauty, splendor, wonder, enlightenment, love, mercy and salvation. Christians are connected through the Holy Spirit within us which is God's temple, His church (a dwelling place of God). If we do not stay in contact with the body of Christ, we are missing the most wonderful experience and the privilege of being a Christian, similar to the case of a University that has numerous scholarships and only a small amount of people applying for them. Paul's comprehension of the revelation of God,

> *"To me, who am less than the least of all the saints, this grace was given, that I should preach among the Gentiles the unsearchable riches of Christ, to the intent that now the manifold wisdom of God might be made known by the church to the principalities and powers in the heavenly places, according to the eternal purpose which He accomplished in Christ Jesus our Lord, in whom we have boldness and access with confidence through faith in Him. Therefore I ask that you do not lose heart at my tribulations for you, which is your glory. Now to Him who is able to do exceedingly abundantly above all that we ask or think, according to the power that works in us, to Him be glory in the church by Christ Jesus to all generations, forever and ever." Eph. 3:8, 10-13, 20-21*

Notice that Paul said, "My tribulations for you, which is your glory." God turns our tribulations to glory and grace for the equipment of the body and to strengthen the members with spiritual authority which is the key for a joyful life. Because we have the power of the Holy Spirit in us, God is able to exceed abundantly above all that we ask or think. God is a great God, so we ought to think great thoughts with confidence, since our thoughts can never be greater than God. We can only marvel at His greatness in how He sustains all things in His universe. His universal authority and power have not diminished in heaven or earth; His is the same yesterday, today and forever. Paul's growing comprehension of the revelation concerning the body of Christ is as fallows,

Christ Our Cornerstone

> *Now, therefore, you are no longer strangers and foreigners, but fellow citizens with saints and members of the household of God. Having been built on the foundation of the apostles and prophets, Jesus Christ Himself being the chief cornerstone, in whom the whole building, being fitted together, grows into a holy temple in the Lord, in whom you also are being built together for a dwelling place of God in the Spirit. Eph. 2:19-22*

Appreciation of the mystery

"For this reason I bow my knees to the Father of our Lord Jesus Christ, from whom the whole family in heaven and earth is named, that He would grant you, according to the riches of His glory, to be strengthened with might through His Spirit in the inner man, that Christ may dwell in your hearts through faith; that you, being rooted and grounded in love, to know the love of Christ which passes knowledge; that you may be filled with all the fullness of God."
Eph. 3:14-17, 19

For the Lord God is a sun and shield; The Lord will give grace and glory; No good thing will He withhold from those who walk uprightly. Psalm 84:11

* * *

The Father's House: The temple of Jehovah in Jerusalem was a permanent building where God manifested His holy presence. There were sacrifices offered by members for their sins. There the priests and servants worshiped and prayed to God for salvation. This place separated God's holiness from the world. Paul called the church at Ephesus **"a Holy Temple."** Now we call His church **"a Dwelling Place of God"** which is the believer's body through baptism, not a house of stone. God dwells in the heart of the believer of Jesus Christ through the Holy Spirit. His temple is composed of believers. Jesus said that he would build His church on Peter's revelation that Jesus was the Son of God; the Messiah. Paul the disciple dispenses the grace of God, the meaning of the church that by revelation was given to him. In other ages this revelation would not have been given to the sons of men, but now through the Holy Spirit, revelations could be given to His apostles and prophets.

That the Gentiles should be fellow heirs, of the same body, and partakers of His promise in Christ through the gospel. Of which I became a minister according to the gift of the grace of God given to me by the effective working of His power. Eph. 3:6-7

There are three indispensable principles that we must practice in order to have the opportunity to accomplish and obtain the riches of the body of Christ.

One... Give Christ an opening for having a relationship with us.

Second... The necessity of having communion with Christians, so we can learn from each other, because we all have different functions.

Third... Doing our part to maintain a strong body; by praying and professing our faith and being obedient to His authority.

These principles sustain the body and give power to its functioning. The activities that vary in each individual make us aware of how important everybody is and how grateful we should be for their contribution of prayer and suffering for the body's glory, grace and power and for the sanctification and justification of the members of the body that Jesus Christ died and suffered to be saved. We are saved by grace alone. Jesus is trying to save as many Christians as possible through His love. He makes His body available like manna. He said, **"I am the bread of life."** Through His body, staying together with faith, we acquire wisdom, calmness, appeasement for our troubles, prosperity for our needs and healing or direction to our healing. **We walk in faith.**

Sustaining the Building: Christ articulates His ministry by calling to all members of the body, not only communities that exercise the rhythm of organized religion, but also nondenominational communities to sustain His church. The time has come to nurture the expansion of these gatherings of Christians that worship and do God's work. Pastors of churches trust in God's divine providence to help His followers and servants who strive to do His purpose and will. When Jesus cleanses the temple, He reminds them that the temple is God's house of prayer.

"It is written," "My house shall be called a house of prayer." Matt. 21:13

The structure of the building of God's church relies strictly on the church members' generosity. Aiding this portion of the body with our resources is important. God then will unite the branches of the vine, exercising His blessings that may be freely shared and enjoyed. We ought to never isolate ourselves, but contribute to these communities of God if we want to be recipients of God's love, grace and gifts. A person who joins a church must recognize that the congregation is required and entrusted with the obligation of helping to bring a steady inflow of goods for the upkeep of the church building. Provisions have to be made for the secure running of the maintenance and repairs of the building, not minimizing the fact of what the affairs of the household require and the administrations' salaries. It is not an obligation to render what is of God to help these organizations, however, it is supposed to be a duty out of the love we have for God and a matter of integrity. We are creating confidence and joy, knowing we are doing God's will.

"Render therefore to Caesar the things that are Caesar's and to God the things that are God's." Matt. 22:21

As Christians we must acknowledge that everything on planet earth belongs to God. All God expects is for us to help each other. By making contributions to the organizations that are doing God's work, we are helping Him too. Also, by helping organizations that build churches, we are involved in creating places where God's people worship and honor Him. Our duty is to show God's glory and give witness to His love and to grow in our oneness as a member of the community in the body of Christ. The church was revealed to Paul and other apostles by the Holy Spirit.

So then each of us shall give account of himself to God. Rom. 14:12

There are certainly no perfect churches, for the demands and yearnings of people are too great to meet. Therefore, we should pray to be guided to a true church for ourselves where we can have enthusiasm for the church's vision. Our main concern and reliance should be to honor and share Jesus' gospel. Nourishing our life in Christ will enable us and others to love communal life in the body of Christ and aids the Christian faith.

"Therefore let us not judge one another anymore, but rather resolve this, not to put a stumbling block or a cause to fall in our brother's way."
Rom. 14:13

Prosperity: Should we expect to be abundantly compensated for helping with contributions to a church, such as blessings and granting petition prayers from God? This seems to be a peculiar American theology that some critics think is used by very popular pastors to make money for themselves. This doctrine is known by various names like **"hard-core prosperity," "name it and claim it"** and **"the word of faith."** Our response to this kind of preaching should first be to ask the Holy Spirit for assistance in discerning the truth, and check how Scripture treats the topic.

There is an article by David Van Biem and Jeff Chu in the September 18, 2006 issue of TIME magazine entitled "Does God Want You to Be Rich?" Yes, say some megachurches. Others call this belief heresy. The debate is heated over the new gospel of wealth. Here are some parts of the article.

Advocates note Prosperity's racial diversity-a welcome exception to the American norm-and point out some Prosperity churches engaging significant in charity. And they are being chastened for their sins than celebrated as God's children. "Who would want to get in on something where you're miserable, poor broke and ugly and you just have to muddle through until you get to heaven?" asks Joyce Meyers, a popular television preacher and author.

"I don't think I've ever preached a sermon about money," Osteen says a few hours later. He and Victoria meet with TIME in their pastoral suite, once the Houston Rocket's locker and shower area but now a zone of overstuffed sofas and imposing oak bookcases. "Does God want us to be rich?" he asks. "When

I hear that word rich, I think people say, Well, he's preaching that everybody is going to be a millionaire.' I don't think that's it." Rather, he explains, "I preach that anybody can improve their lives. I think God wants us to be prosperous. I think he wants us to be happy. To me, you need to have money to pay your bills. I think God wants us to send our kids to college. I think he wants us be a blessing to other people. But I don't think I'd say God wants us to be rich. It's all relative, isn't it?"The room's warm lamplight reflects softly off his crocodile shoes.

***

We are inclined to be critical of Osteen, Creflo Dollar, Joyce Meyer and their spouses' work, ignoring the tremendous dedication it takes to maintain their members' satisfaction or to notice how hard these preachers work to sustain a congregation the size of so called megachurches. One can only imagine that God has to be on their side because they are able to keep all of these people satisfied with their preaching and the way they run the church. It is unfair to criticize these pastors with big congregations and not give them credit for the intense and difficult work they do for God. To help fuel enthusiasm about the Christian faith and help a big number of people believe and trust the Lord takes divine supernatural intervention. Pastors who preach about prosperity base their beliefs on the verse that Jesus said,

"I have come that they may have life, and have it abundantly," John 10:10

There are pastors who find prosperity theology a simplistic philosophy and embarrassing to believe,

"It is easier for a camel to go through the eye of a needle than for a rich man to enter the kingdom of God." Mark 10:25

The Bible leaves plenty of room for the discussion of the subject of money. There is information in the Bible about the role of money and the positive and negative effects. This is when we need to pray for discernment, for God to give us the ability to separate truth from erroneous theology. The Holy Spirit will allow us the grace to know the will of God. Discernment will help us to focus on what is important to listen to and whom to avoid.

Anton has two sons. One would love to have crocodile shoes, while the other one could not be paid enough to wear crocodile shoes; however, she loves them both the same. Anybody who has several children can understand this concept. This is exactly how the Father is. He loves us all the same, whether we like luxuries or not. In fact, He is pleased when we own things that make us happy, as long as we do not forget the needy. Paul the disciple said, **"Money is the root of all evil."** That is true when we let money possess us, because money can become our master. Unfortunately, we need money to live, but it should always be our servant, not our master.

It is unfair to criticize pastors who are successful in their parishes, instead of recognizing the dedication, imagination and devotion it takes to develop the confidence of the followers of the Lord. God is pleased and will bless His servants who help fuel and spread His word. It is not our job to worry or point our finger at pastors who take advantage of their position in the church. They are the bad apples in the body of Christ and He will deal with them and will expose them in His time. Addressing this subject requires prayer for the Holy Spirit to guide us to the truth.

Understanding His Word: It was mentioned earlier that God is not a respecter of persons. He is meticulous and considerate of our different characteristics.

Then Peter opened his mouth and said "God shows no partiality." Acts 10:34

There is a reason for the various relationships with His children. We are uniquely made; therefore, His relationship is not equivalent. There is a certain asymmetry about it. He focuses on a person's life and sensitivity to perceive information. Consequently, He has to select different prophets to administer His word, because we all require different techniques and methods to understand His word. What may be profound preaching to one person may not be to the other person. Some Christians need the enthusiasm and positive preaching of the **"word of faith."** It helps them to believe in themselves and to deal with the struggles of life. They need the encouragement and to learn to appreciate their value in Christ.

There has to be an acquirement of the fullness of God in order for a person not to be deceived by false prophets. The Spirit abiding in us is the Immanent (existing and extending into the entire universe) Creator of all things manifesting Himself though us. The manifestation of the reality of the Creator living in us depends on our ability to accept and recognize the truth. His sanctification and justification will manifest in us when we have the recognition and the trust of His divine presence, which is His Immanent Holiness. His divine life is always perfect, strong and vigorous in us, and through prayer it will flow to our circumstances. Helping us to discern what is acceptable for our life, experiencing physical recognition and acceptance of God's will. It is so wonderful to reach this state of consciousness, because it gives us a loving understanding of other Christian's requirements. Without being critical and judgmental, we feel compassionate and recognize that we all have different needs in our spiritual walk.

Our main purpose is to find the right organization that will feed our spirit with enthusiasm and excitement over God's word, connecting and leading us toward a vision of being One with the Father. Then the Father will plant a seed of deep enjoyment. He will awake our inner purpose with vibrational frequency difficult to explain. Creative ability and imagination will enhance and lead us to a better life. No matter what circumstances in which we find ourselves, our structural balance will remain intact. God's empowerment will guide us to conquer difficult and adverse situations. Embracing and recognizing God's word will activate our senses to captivate His presence and His constant helping hand in our journey.

"GOD'S KINGDOM IS AT HAND."

* * *

What you see passes; but the invisible, that which is not seen, does not pass; it remains. Behold, it is received: it is eaten; it is consumed. Is the body of Christ consumed? Is the church consumed? Are the members consumed? God for-bid! Here they are cleansed; there they will be crowned. Therefore, what is signified will last eternally, even though it seems to pass. Receive, then, so that you may ponder, so that you may possess unity in your heart, so that you may always lift up your heart.

Augustine

Persecuted Woman

The symbolic representation of a woman clothed with the sun in Revelations has mystified scholars as to what the actual signification means.

Now a great sign appeared in heaven: a woman clothed with the sun, with the moon under her feet, and on her head a garland of twelve stars. And another sign appeared in heaven: behold, a great, fiery red dragon having seven heads and ten horns, and seven diadems on his head. He persecuted the woman who gave birth to the male-child. Rev. *12:1, 3, 13*

This woman is with child and in labor crying out in the agony of giving birth. Some scholars perceive her as the symbolic representation of Israel, since the Messiah came from Israeli people. Supposedly, the twelve stars on her head are the twelve tribes of Israel. Then, there are scholars who clearly see this as a symbol of God's people on earth (the church). The woman who gives birth to the man-child signifies the battle of bringing God's kingdom to earth. The sun represents Christ and God's people on earth, and the moon signifies the night age which is the Old Testament, the age of the law. The stars on her head are symbols of the patriarchs which are the Biblical ancestors. Early Christian writers thought the symbol of the woman represented Mary. Some think it also could be the church, since it states in Rev. of having other children, which could be the members of the church. The dragon is the enemy trying to devour the Christians. The reason for all the speculations is because the precise identity of this woman is unknown.

The Lord gave John the apostle revelations that consisted of a series of panoramic visions that revealed the past, present and future, but it is literal and figurative; a mystery.

"I am the Alpha and the Omega, the first and last." Rev. *1:11*

* * *

Aztec Princess: In Mexico there was an apparition of a lady on December 12, 1531 that left a print of the image of a Lady on a tilma (a garment worn by the Aztec Indians) belonging to Juan Diego. Juan was a new convert to the Christian faith at that time. The fabric of the tilma is so thin that people can see through it, but this same fabric has not deteriorated in more then 475 years. The sparkling colors are still bright and the image has a supreme loveliness about it. Numerous experts have expressed their wonderment at the image's preservation from all the opposing elements of time and decay. A picture containing the tilma is located at the Basilica of Guadalupe in Mexico City. It is encased in a frame made of solid gold.

The Lady on the tilma is presented as if she is an Aztec princess. She is looking down modestly with her head slightly tilted to the right. Her hands are folded at her breast, showing devotion to One greater than her and showing she also prays and supplicates. She is wearing a bluish-marine colored robe that resembles a gala dress of an Aztec princess. The cape has 46 golden stars and also covers her head. Her tunic is pinkish with a touch of salmon color and with a floral design of gold embroidery. On her waist there is a band representing cloistering of an infant and alluding to her motherhood. On her neck, at her throat, there is a small golden brooch, impressed on its surface. a black cross. It is unmistakably the same design carried on the banner of Hernando Cortez, representing the true faith that Jesus Christ is the only pleasing Divine sacrifice for the sins of the world. This also, was made clear to the Indians by the Miraculous Picture of the Lady.

OUR GOD IS THE CREATOR AND MASTER

OF DETAILS. ALL WE HAVE TO DO IS LOOK AT

CREATION TO REALIZE THE MAGNIFICENT PLAN

THAT GOD INITIATED THROUGH HIS LOVE.

These Indians had been worshiping the sun, but with the apparition of this Lady there was everything. There is a full splendor surrounding her, as if the sun is behind her and radiant rays, straight and drizzly. There are one hundred and twenty-nine rays jetting out, enveloping her figure to form a golden border of splendor and brilliance. She is wearing a crown of ten lancelets that are brilliant too. This is just like the Bible reveals to us, that we might attain a crown for our good works if we go to heaven. **"The imperishable crown"** 1Cor. 9:25 She is standing on the moon with an angel holding the crescent. The angel is wearing a bluish-green tunic. His wings are white with a pinkish touch. There have been two commissioned studies conducted on different occasions where experts intensely examined the image. Nothing goes undetected in the picture. The angel is also wearing a brooch, but without the cross. Perhaps, because unlike man; the angels were not redeemed by Jesus Christ.

These children of nature were quick to understand the message of the Lady blotting out the sun. The Redeemer was greater than this heavenly body to which they were offering human sacrifices. He had sent His Mother carrying Him and, not only that, but the sun and the stars adorned her cape and the angel held the moon at her feet. Jesus was the real God. They were also greatly impressed with the cross Mary was wearing. They exulted and were compelled to embrace the true faith of Jesus Christ that Hernando Cortez's missionaries had talked to them about.

The Indians were so appreciative that this beautiful, sweet and kind Lady, who was the earthly mother of Jesus, had come to show them the way to salvation, that they decided to adopt her as their mother too. This is the reason why most people from Mexico are so devoted to the Virgin Mary.

The Mexican people accepted the apparition as Mary the mother of Jesus who represented the Immaculate Conception. The ribbon around her waist signified that she was with child; Jesus Christ. It was as if she was telling them, **"Stop killing your Children. My Son has already sacrificed His life for you all."** Most of these Indians were pagans worshiping gods, the sun, the stars, the moon, plants, and animals. They offered as many as 20,000 human sacrifices annually. These poor Indians fell victims to the sacrificial knife of their pagan priests. Cortez and his valiant Christians missionaries could not break the reign of Montezuma and stop this inhuman system. God used Mary to charm these Aztec Indians with her gentleness, tenderness and unparalleled graciousness in her dealing with Juan Diego. This enraptured and captured their hearts. They interpreted the picture step by step. It is a historical fact that some 8,000.000 or more literally flooded the Christian church within eight years. God's use of Mary succeeded much more than Cortez could to convert these deluded souls to Christianity.

There is a book about the apparition of Mary that makes a few observations. The book's title is THAT MOTHERLY MOTHER OF GUADALUPE by L.M. Dooley, S.V.D.

An observation registered by all is this one: the Miraculous Image seems to assume a reversal of size and color quite contrary to any other normal experience in the examination of pictures.

Normally, we know, the very opposite is the case: at closer range details are noted, and greater distance they fade into insignificance. One notes, secondly, a sense of Mary's Presence.

Regarding the unique and tremendous sense of Presence, felt almost universally by all, permit this quotation by an honored and cherished friend, Coley Taylor, co author of the well documented and authentic work, "The Dark Virgin" (Demarest and Taylor). The following is an extract from a letter which he wrote to Rt. Reverend Father Columbian, O.C.S.O. From it we quote:

"A magnetic graciousness that has never been my experience with any other painting, religious or secular, that I have over admired and loved, lingers there, and I have seen and studied and admired so many masterpieces in my twenty-five years in New York: El Grecos, Goyas, Leonardos, Michaelangelos, Rafaels, Verneers, Holbeins, Rembrandts, Raeburns, Titians, in the permanent collections in the museums, in private collection, and great loan exhibitions from the World's Fair. There is nothing comparable to Our Lady's Portrait. She left something of her presence with it, that is all I can say ... And it is this gentle presence, this vivacious graciousness, this enigmatical radiance that no artist, nor any reproduction can capture.

* * *

In TIME magazine on March 21, 2005, an article on Mary by David Van Biema, "Hail, Mary," reveals how Catholics have long revered her, but now Protestants are finding their own reasons to celebrate the earthly mother of Jesus. This is part of the report,

Rev. Brian Maguire, a 35-year-old pastor's brainstorm concerned a scheduling conflict on the day of the Annunciation. The holiday, which celebrates Mary's learning from the angel Gabriel that she will give birth to the Messiah, always falls on March 25, precisely nine months before Christmas. But this year the 25th is also Good Friday, when Christians somberly recall that same Messiah's Crucifixion. Roman Catholicism, which traditionally observes both dates, has rules for this eventually; Catholics worldwide will mark the Annunciation on April 4 this year. But Maguire is not Catholic; he is the pastor of West minster Presbyterian Church in Xenia, Ohio. And in light of what he calls "a beautiful, poetic opportunity," he says that rather than preach on Jesus alone this Good Friday, he will bring in Mary as well. "If you have Jesus' entrance and exit on the same day," Maguire explains, "she should play a part in that-because she was the first and last disciple to reach out during His life."

The same article in TIME magazine mentions about a shift of ideological breath in the Protestant world. It appears a long standing wall around Mary is beginning to erode. Protestants are not exalting Mary dramatically in the same manner as Catholics, but it appears they are taking notice of her important part in Jesus' life. It is not that they are turning into Catholic thinkers, but they are taking notice of the information in the Bible. This is part of the paragraph,

Rather, a growing number of Christian thinkers who are neither Catholic nor Eastern Orthodox. (Another branch of faith to Mary is central) have concluded that their various traditions have short-changed her in the very arena in which Protestantism most prides itself: the careful and full reading of Scripture.

* * *

It was stated in the beginning of the book that different subjects were going to be addressed, and this one is controversial with Protestants. Anton came from a protestant background and did not understand her Catholic husband's devotion to the Virgin Mary. Now, with her private revelations, she could settle this fundamental theological matter. She asked the Holy Spirit how God perceived this notion of praying to Mary. The Holy Spirit's vibrations answered, **"In heaven there is no conflict or animosity, only unity, love and harmony."** She realized her question was unfounded, because God is not in heaven condemning us for our ignorance or acknowledgement of His word. On the contrary, He is full of love, compassion and understanding for the human race. He will use any resources available to Him to assist us in our every day life. There are people that need a sweet and strong female role model in church. And who better than Jesus' earthly mother, a biblical figure that can encourage their speculations in their lives. God will not leave them without witness. Paul the disciple talked of the goodness of the living God,

"Who in bygone generations allowed all nations to walked
in their own ways. Nevertheless He did not leave Himself without witness,
in that He did good, gave us rain from heaven and fruitful seasons, filling our

hearts with food and gladness." Acts 14:16-17

The redeemer was born through the Virgin Mary, God's vessel of honor. God knew Jesus would be in good hands. He gave her grace and strength for this intricate plan. With her humility, obedience and submissiveness to God's will, we gain what was lost with Adam and Eve in the Paradise of God. Paradise is a place that symbolizes the eschatological state where men had a perfect fellowship with God before Satan entered the world. Now all Christians have the same opportunity as before to have fellowship with God through the Holy Spirit.

The Virgin is an important part of scripture. God used her as a channel to obtain Jesus' birth on earth. When Jesus was born, God took physical human form in His Son. It is all so miraculous that the human mind has difficulty understanding such disclosure. Only through faith can we comprehend this divine simple idea of reality, that God discloses Himself through His Son.

Mary must have the most beautiful crown in heaven for her mission. She was very important in Jesus' life. She was the one that helped at the wedding in Cana of Galilee. That's when Jesus turned the water into wine, His first miracle. He did this somewhat grudgingly, at the insistence of His Mother. Jesus said to her,

"Woman what does your concern have to do with me? My hour has not yet come." His mother said to the servants, "Whatever He says to you, do it." John 2:4-5

She was the only woman named at the gathering of the disciples in the upper room in Jerusalem, where the first supernatural manifestation ministry of the Holy Spirit came upon them and the power from heaven as promised by Jesus. The mighty outpouring of power transformed their lives and ignited the life of the church, all in one, the body of Christ.

When the day of Pentecost had fully come they were all with one accord in one place. Acts 2:1

The Holy Spirit is Jesus and God all three in one, and He is the only intermediary to the spiritual realm. We need Jesus first to reach Mary, which is significantly opposite compared to the usual belief. Christians have the Holy Spirit living within. Jesus said,

"I am with you always, even to the end of the age." Matt. 28:20

"He who has seen Me has seen the Father. Do you not believe Me that I am in the Father and the Father in Me? The words that I speak to you I do not speak on My own Authority." John 14:9-10

The theory and explanation to this equation makes sense. We need Jesus first to reach Mary; then, this sanctified lady will pray for us through intercessory prayer and guide us back to Jesus. Most sons are very protective of their mothers. Jesus is not going to expose the light of her heart of a mother to shine on somebody that does not need her. But, He is ready to assist the believer that needs female comforting and prayer. When we call on Mary, she is right there in a split second. In the infinite, there is no time or space.

Jesus has the ultimate respect and love for this dear humble and obedient spirit of God. There are Christians that see no wrong doing in asking for support from Mary. Jesus also relied on support from His disciples. He did this to show us that interaction is very important. There are people who do not limit themselves to prayers from only the physical realm, they rely on prayers from the spiritual realm to. Mary is a sanctified spirit, and the prayer of the righteous is very powerful. Paul stated,

While we do not look at things which are seen, but at things which are not seen. For the things which are seen are temporary, but the things which are not seen are eternal. 2 Cor. 4:18

Jesus said to the disciples,

> *"Assuredly, I say to you, whatever you bind on earth will be bound in heaven, and whatever you loose on earth will be loosed in heaven."* Matt. 18:18

We have to be firm with our beliefs here on earth for them to work in the spirit realm. The spiritual realm is interchangeable and interwoven with the physical realm. We are actually living and existing in both realms. We need to see with our spiritual eyes to be able to perceive and benefit from both spectrums.

BEING A CHRISTIAN IS BELIEVING IN CHRIST AND

THROUGH THIS BELIEF EVERYTHING IS POSSIBLE.

Ingrid Betancourt is an example of having the consolation of Mary's presence at her side when she was captive in the Colombian jungle for over five years. This is the information she shared with the public when she was rescued by 'Colombia Hostage Rescue.' God was not going to leave this brave woman without witness. She found herself in the middle of male captors and, of course, she needed the company of a female spirit. Ingrid was kidnapped by F.A.R.C. on February 23, 2002 when she was running for the presidency of Colombia and rescued on July 3, 2008.

* * *

When Jesus was being crucified, He saw His mother and His beloved disciple John standing by the cross. Then He said to His mother,

> *"Woman, behold your son!" Then He said to the disciple, "Behold your mother!"* John 19:26-27

Anton held this verse close to her heart. What a wonderful mystic opportunity this was to adopt Mary as our mother, especially if we were not blessed with a kind, loving mother.

We think of Mary when we hear of mothers losing their sons and daughters in war. She had to endure the pain of seeing her Son give up His life for the good of the world. These mothers are doing the exactly the same thing.

Keeping things in perspective, we should never think we are being disrespectful when we do not honor or acknowledge Mary. She worships Jesus, and that is all she wants from the rest of us; she appreciates the love we have for her Son. Anybody who is a mother will recognize this aspect, that a mother will step aside for her children's recognition. Love is the most powerful emotion; it is carried beyond this life.

* * *

When you find yourself wanting to turn your children, or pupils, or even your neighbors, into people exactly like yourself, remember that God probably never meant them to be that. You and they are different organs, intended to do different things. On the other hand, when you are tempted not to bother about someone else's troubles because they are 'no business of yours' remember that though he is different from you he is part of the same organism as you. If you forget that he belongs to the same organism as yourself you will become an Individualist. If you forget that he is a different organ from you, if you want to suppress differences and make people all alike, you will become a Totalitarian. But a Christian must not be either a Totalitarian or an Individualist.

C.S. Lewis

Hear , O Lord And have mercy on me; Lord be my helper! You have turned for me my mourning into dancing; You have put off my sackcloth and clothed me with gladness, To the end that my glory may sing praise to You and not be silent. O Lord my God, I will give thanks to You forever.
Ps. 30:10-12

Bearing Fruit

Being a disciple means to be a positive person, ready to be a witness and to serve the church. A disciple experiences the power of the Spirit.

"Behold, I send the promise of My Father upon you; but tarry in the city of Jerusalem until you are endued with the power from on high." Luke 24:49

Pam helped Anton for two hours, once a week, for approximately two years. She examined and typed the notes Anton had written by hand containing information about what she considered could help Christians in their walk of faith. She also examined theological reflections on concepts that could lead individuals to experience a deeper relationship with the Lord. Anton presented Pam her ideas according to the mysteries of her humble seeking of the Holy Spirit's guidance. She was honestly amazed in the constant invitation the Lord has for us to unite with Him that is beyond our existence and knowledge. If Pam did not understand the notes, then Anton would verbally try to explain her intentions. In return, Pam typed the information, sometimes correcting Anton's expressions. Because the language barrier, it was difficult for Anton to sort out exactly of what she was trying to convey. This was mentioned before that when we perceive information through the Holy Spirit's vibrations, our brain translates it into our own perception and reasoning. Anton was so excited about the information she was receiving, but she had a difficult time expressing it exactly the way she perceived it. An example, **"The basic quest is to acquire an adequate disposition of the Holy Spirit. From there we will understand His emotions and inner attitudes, which will lead us to the inner atmosphere of Jesus, capturing the inner harmony of the Lord."** We can see the importance of the message, so that anybody trying to be apostolic has to be careful with the proper words and expressions.

Ignacio Larrañaga , author of Sensing Your Hidden Presence, wrote,

Speaking from within Jesus

Those who *sense* this, will have to go out from the valley of contemplation to communicate something of what they "saw and heard." This is an essential task of true worshippers: to speak (or write) as someone who speaks from within Jesus, after having participated, in the spirit and faith, in the profound experience of the Lord. It is an extraordinary difficult but necessary task.

Among all human experience, prayer is the most profound and far-reaching. And now that we want to speak of Jesus' prayer, I am aware that we cannot utter a single word without the aid of the Holy Spirit, which we ardently request.

* * *

The idea here is to promote vocal prayers that we can present to the Lord, He is not distant or beyond reach. Getting rid of distractions that so often cloud our minds is the only psychological way to silence and quiet the senses, so the presence of God can flourish into a wonderful fellowship. The deep and living fountain is not that far; in fact, it is within us. Prayer will give us faith and our love will intensify giving us the sureness of His presence. Thus, we will not see Him since He does not have a form, but clarity is the perception of a living God that is alive. He is accessible, compatible, and personally within reach. Being able to have a dialogue with the Lord of the universe, gives us the notion that we have arrived to the highest point of our life, capturing the inner harmony of God. Seeking the mystery of Jesus will give us the power of the Holy Spirit and the knowledge of the utter fullness of God. Paul the disciple said,

May you be able to comprehend with all the saints what
is the width and length and depth and height to know the love

of Christ which passes knowledge; that you may be filled with all the fullness of God. Eph. 3:18-19

O lamps of fire! In whose splendors the deep caverns of feeling Once obscure and blind, Now give forth, so rarely, so exquisitely, both warmth and light to their Beloved.

John of the Cross

When the Samaritan woman met Jesus at Jacob's well, she was surprised that He knew everything she ever did in her life. She wondered if He could be the Messiah.

The woman said to Him, "Sir, I perceive that You are a prophet. Our fathers worshiped on this mountain, and you Jews say that Jerusalem is the place where one ought to worship." Jesus said to her, "Woman, believe Me, the hour is coming when you will neither on this mountain, nor in Jerusalem, worship the Father. But the hour is coming, and now is, when the true worshipers will worship the Father in spirit and truth; for the Father is seeking such to worship Him. God is Spirit, and those who worship Him must worship in spirit and truth." John 4:19-21, 23-24.

Jesus foretold the future of the Christian's dispensation, in which we worship in spirit and truth. The Samaritans only accepted and believe part of the Old Testament, the Pentateuch which is Genesis and Deuteronomy. They did not have the whole truth of God. Most of the Jews did possess the real truth of the true God, but Sadducees denied the supernatural and the resurrection and the Pharisees were so legalist (religious); they were strict with their religion and their interpretations of the laws. They did not worship in spirit.

However, the presence of God is not so easily perceived by all Christians. Nevertheless, God is there within us and we can worship and pray at anytime we desire. We are so fortunate that sometimes we take it for granted and ignore God. Anton is talking of herself. She realizes that if she had never started to pray the Lords Prayer at night, she never would have experienced the wonderful encounter with the Lord. The only reason she prayed was to be assured of her immortality because we all are going to die sometime. And just in case, that there really is a heaven she wanted to have the opportunity of salvation. Since the Lord's Prayer has the petition for the forgiveness of our sins, she would get to the pearly gates clean of sin.

We are God's beloved. He dwells within us. When we abide in the mystery of God, then we truly become able to experience the overwhelming reality of his presence. When we search in the central part of our being, thus discovering the presence of the Lord we will also find our own true selves--- in Christ, sensing a personal union with Him. We revolutionize our entire inner being with the desire to submerge ourselves in the fundamental approach to Christian truths and switch our interest to Bible stories. We displace our worries for external cultural values, concentrating on prayer and realizing the importance of our spiritual journey, which is accepting Christ's invitation to a spiritual life that is in alignment with God's purpose, even considering the idea of studying a vocation to serve God. For example, a retired military man is now a Methodist Pastor and a travel agent acquired her degree in Creative Writing and now writes stories for her church.

Anton is inspired to work for the Lord too. He has given us unique spiritual gifts to use in what He calls us to do or be in this world for that particular assignment. Jesus told us how important it is to abide in Him and **bear fruit.**

"If you abide in Me, and My words abide in you, you will ask what you desire, and it shall be done for you. By this My Father is glorified, that you bear much fruit; so you will be My disciples."
John 15:7-8

The spiritual life can be lived in as many ways as there are people. What is new is that we have moved from the many things to the kingdom of God. What is new is that we are set free from the compulsion of our world and have set our hearts on the only necessary thing.

Henri J.M. Nouwen

When we recognize the truthfulness of God, we want to please and serve Him with all our heart, but sometimes obstacles keep getting in the way. Anton found herself in a predicament. She had accumulated notes for over two years to be a witness for the Lord; however, she had nobody to type even the beginning of the book. The reason was that her good friend Pam, who so kindly helped her write the notes, had become ill. Her poor physical health prevented her from doing everything she wanted to do. For example, she came down with Carpal Tunnel Syndrome on both of her wrists and found it impossible to type until she had surgery to relieve the terrible pain. After an operation on her wrists, she began to feel better. Then she developed cancer on the right side of her face. Her doctors recommended surgery to remove the cancer, followed by painful radiation to burn off any cancerous cells left behind.

Anton is faced with hardship, because of her predicament. She now has an understanding of God's word, but she has nobody to type her beliefs for her. Pam is incapacitated and is not able to help her anymore. The vibrations of the Holy Spirit let her know that she could type her own material. She remembered that she had the computer He recommended for her to buy. She must learn to operate it. She thought, **"Okay, I will give it a try."** Only some people over 60 years old can relate to this concept, because computers were not from our era. To her amazement and surprise she started to type as if it was second nature to her, as if she had always typed. Only when she would try to memorize where the keys were located did she have trouble. If she did not think about what she was doing, then it was as if somebody else was guiding her hands. And for some strange reason, she felt closer to the Lord when she was typing. If she was not sure of an expression, she would ask the Holy Spirit, and He would move her head to a yes or a no. If there was no movement, then she would ask Him to put a different thought in her head. It was so fantastic that she herself had a hard time analyzing it and believing it. But with God's help anything and everything is possible. Even though Anton is receiving assistance from the Holy Spirit, it is still her perception and her thoughts. After all, we are God's voice and hands in this world

But in all things we commend ourselves as ministers of God: in much patience, in tribulations, in needs, in distresses, in stripes, in imprisonments, in tumults, in labors, in sleeplessness, in fasting; by purity, by knowledge, by long suffering, by kindness, by the Holy Spirit, by sincere love. 2 Cor. 6:4-6

It is quite understandable that in a large anonymous city we look for people on our "wave length" to form small communities. But sometimes a false type of like-mindedness can narrow our sense of community. There is a great wisdom hidden in the old bell tower calling people with different backgrounds away from their homes to form one body in Jesus Christ. It is precisely by transcending the many individual differences that we can become witnesses of God who allows His light to shine upon poor and rich, healthy and sick alike.

Henri J.M. Nouwen

Now then, we are ambassadors for Christ, as though God is pleading through us: we implore you on Christ's behalf, be reconciled with God. 2 Cor. 5:20

Being God's voice and hands makes us His representatives. That responsibility takes courage and confidence that comes from within. After Jesus' ascension, Peter and John were sharing their faith with a council of elders and teachers in Jerusalem. These members were amazed at the confidence these men demonstrated. They knew they were ordinary men who had no special education or training. Therefore, the members recognized that it was God that was creating the confidence in Peter and John. They had learned not to trust their own limited capacity, but rather to trust the abilities of the Lord who worked through them through the Holy Spirit. This is obtained by waking in the Spirit; which is having God in mind at all times. There is a part of Peter's sermon, after he received the Holy Spirit, that says,

"This Jesus God has raised up, of which we are all witnesses. Therefore being exalted to the right hand of God, and having received from the Father the promise of the Holy Spirit, He poured out this which you now see and hear." Acts 2:32-33

We are all so fortunate now to have received the Holy Spirit through baptism. The Holy Spirit resides in our heart. All we have to do is engage the mind too. It was mentioned before that in the Old Testament only a few had the Holy Spirit within and a young man named David happened to be one. David is an example of what one can do with faith and the grace of God. The story of David and Goliath shows how this young man, a shepherd with a slingshot, faced the giant who wanted to feed his flesh to the birds and wild animals. David had courage, because he knew God wanted him to engage in this battle. David used his slingshot with confidence and said, **"I come to you in the name of the Lord Almighty."**

Then David put his hands in his bag and took out a stone; and he slung it and stuck the Philistine in the forehead, so that the stone sank into his forehead, and he fell on his face to the earth. So David prevailed over the Philistine with a sling and a stone, and struck the Philistine and killed him. 1 Sam. 17:49-50

So David went on, and became great, and the Lord God of hosts was with him. 2 Sam. 5:10

God works in mysterious ways. When we are obedient to God's commands He will mysteriously assist us with convenient circumstances and special people emerging in our lives who will make a great impact on our lives with help and encouragement for the purpose and task God has put in our hearts. This usually happens quite unexpectedly and surprisingly and is an example of God's providence and grace. When we are trying to accomplish a task, if we do it in the name of the Lord with conviction, it will bring integrity to the project and credibility to whatever we are trying to convey.

It is God who arms me with
strength, and makes my way perfect. Ps. 18:32

And the Lord will make you the head, and not
the tail; you shall be above only, and not be beneath, if you
heed My commandments of the Lord. Deut. 28:13

God can predestine a person or a group of people for service and/or salvation. This is not based on merit, but on His sovereign love. The Jews were God's chosen people. He would reveal Himself and His will to them. Through them He would exhibit and declare to the world His purposes and salvation. Jesus was a Jew who was predestined to be the cornerstone of the new building (the church) that God constructed and composed of both Jewish and Gentile believers. Thank God that Jesus complied and fallowed through with God's plan for the Gentiles.

The chosen stone and His Chosen people: Coming to Him as to a
Living stone, rejected indeed by men, but chosen by God and precious, you also,
a living stones, are being built up a spiritual house, a holy priesthood, to offer up
spiritual sacrifices acceptable to God through Jesus Christ. 1 Peter 2:4-5

"These things I have spoken to you, that in Me you may
have peace. In the world you will have tribulation: but be of
good cheer, I have overcome the world." John 16:33

The chosen people have to decide whether to be obedient to God's will or not. There are individuals that God elects for special roles and tasks. A flowing decision within us is initiated by God and the reaction is our choice to follow through. God's election is never forceful, but rather a kind invitation with love to do His will. He is extremely respectful of the free will that He granted us when chosen in Christ before the foundation of the world. God told Job that he actually was born before He laid the foundation of the earth, Job 38:21. Christians also existed before the foundation, because we were written in the Lamb's Book of life.

Only those who are written in the Lamb's book of life.
Rev. 21:27

That we should be holy and without blame before Him in love, having predestined us to adoption as sons by Jesus Christ to Himself, according to the good pleasure of His will.
Eph. 1:4-5

When we agree to do God's will, a feeling of wholeness and serenity will flow into many areas of our life, a quantum leap forward to our spiritual life, well equipped with discernment and enlightenment. We will understand the importance of introducing and promoting the name of the Lord. This rich environment of our spiritual life will produce great love in our heart transcending us to spiritual wisdom and a sensory impression of His mystery. David spoke to the Lord these words, when delivered from his enemies,

"The Lord is my rock, and my fortress, and my deliverer."
2 Sam. 22:2

For the Lord, hast made me glad through Your work: I will triumph in the works of Your hands.
Ps. 92:4

When Anton was finishing the book, people asked her what kind of great finale she planned for the end of the book. She would responded, **"There's no great finale in a spiritual book. This book is a humble personal story of my relationship with the Lord. It is actually my testimony about how I now recognize that the Lord was mysteriously working in all of my life experiences."** It feels magnificent to realize that God is always present, even when we feel alone. What a wonderful gift to have the realization of the insights of the equation of the body of Christ and realize the reasons for the tribulations in our lives. Our hurts are deposited in the church, a body where all members are eventually honored. Our pain and good deeds are our contributions that eventually turn into blessings by the power of the Lord. God is always in control of our situations and uses bad situations that turn into grace for the salvation of sinners made possible by the blood of Jesus. We are heirs of Jesus' inheritances; we have joined His reign. Anton says, **"I am so appreciative of how fortunate I am that the Lord has revealed Himself to His humble servant; precisely the reason I feel it is my duty to share this message."** There is never enough time to learn everything; not even theologians know everything there is to know about God. Anything we can do to further the kingdom of God will bring strength, exaltation, splendor, mercy to the church; **glory to God in the highest.**

If there was a great finale for this book, it would have to be Martha Lou for coming to Anton's rescue. She needed assistance to finish the book. It was of great help that she could type, but she still needed the appropriate person to proofread her manuscript. She tried not to worry, having confidence that the Lord would find somebody. One day, while at work, she asked Martha Lou, a long time customer of the business, for the proper usage of a particular word. Martha Lou responded that she would have to see how the word was being used in the writing. Anton showed her some of her writing, and she offered to help her with the book. Anton could hardly believe it! This sweet lady was willing to give her valuable time. She could not think of a more qualified person than this good Christian. It had to be God's providence. Martha Lou happened to be her daughter's former high school teacher. She also had worked at the University of Texas at El Paso. She taught English Composition for several years. The beauty of all this is that she did not ask Anton to prove to her why she thought the Holy Spirit was communicating with her through vibrations. This is the kind of person she is, very respectful of other people's beliefs and with a big heart that makes her a **"wonderful human being."**

Faith in divine Providence is the faith that nothing can prevent us from fulfilling the ultimate meaning of our existence. Providence does not mean a divine planning by

which everything is predetermined, as is an effective machine. Rather, Providence means that there is a creative and saving possibility, which cannot be destroyed by any event. Providence means that the daemonic and destructive forces within ourselves and our world can never have an unbreakable grasp upon us, and that the bond which connects us with the fulfilling love can never be disrupted.

Paul Tillich

* * *

Anton wants to encourage Christians to write their testimonies of the relationship they have with the Lord and become His witness. She was inspired by Rick Warren when he suggested in his book, The Purpose Driven Life, in the chapter, **"Sharing Your Life Message,"** that we should write about our relationship with Jesus, our life lessons, our passions and the good news of salvation. He states, that our essence of our message should be simple; we must share our personal experiences regarding the Lord and not worry about who is going to believe us. Our job is to simply report our unique life experiences and the knowledge we have acquired through our faith. He mentions, we do not have to be a Bible scholar, only truthful with our personal experiences with the Lord. He says, **"As a satisfied customer."** Pastor Warren also points out, that by sharing our story it will build a relational bridge that Jesus can walk across from our heart to other people's hearts. He also says, **"There isn't enough time to learn everything in life by trial an error. We must learn from the life lessons of one another."** He mentions that perhaps, we could avoid somebody's frustrations in their lives by knowing our personal life experiences and lessons.

Rick Warren says, **"God is a passionate God. He passionately *loves* some things and passionately *hates* other things. As we grow closer to him, he will give you a passion for something he cares about deeply so you can be a spokesman for him in the world."**

* * *

Anton's concern is to help young people to stay in school. There many students that who never graduate from high school. This will affect them for the rest of their lives. Studies have shown that young adults with low education will likely depend on government assistance longer than those with at least a high school diploma. We need to take notice of the problem and try to make a difference for better communities. These young people need to know that God cares for them and that everybody matters to Him.

Anton wants and hopes to be some sort of help to assist these young people who have trouble in school. Perhaps, after this book is published, God will guide her in the direction of what He wants her to do. As it was mentioned before eighty percent of the proceeds of the book will go to help this "Silent Epidemic" of high school dropouts. It is so difficult to imagine 30% do not graduate from high school and 50% for Hispanics and African Americans.

The author hopes the readers have been touched by the magnificent glimpse into the nature of God that has not often been presented in our society. Perhaps, they would like to help reach a broader audience by purchasing more books as gifts to relatives, friends and even strangers in order to share the good news about how God relates to humanity. This will also encourage Christians who have not yet recognized His assistance and work in their lives, and even those who have already recognized His presence. It will be much appreciated if the reader could recommend the book which is the most effective tool for a book like this to gain attention.

"Again , the kingdom of heaven is like a treasure hidden in a field" Matt. 13:44"Whatever I tell you in the dark, speak in the light; and what you hear in the ear, preach on the housetops." Matt. 10:27

God bless,
--Anton
www.holyspiritinyou.com

*Give me understanding, and I shall keep Your law'
Indeed, I shall observe it with my heart. Make me walk in the path
of Your commandments, For I delight in it. Incline my heart to Your
testimonies, And not to covetousness. Turn away my eyes from looking at
worthless things, And revive me in Your way. Ps. 119:34-37*

CPSIA information can be obtained at www.ICGtesting.com
Printed in the USA
LVOW090309160712

290200LV00006B/131/P

9 781425 181635